Unabashed Faith

Unabashed Faith

Resisting Anti-Spiritual Influences in the Modern World

C. ANDREW DOYLE

Church Publishing
19 East 34th Street
New York, NY 10016

Cover design by David Baldeosingh Rotstein
Typeset by Nord Compo

ISBN 978-1-64065-785-4 (hardcover)
ISBN 978-1-64065-786-1 (ebook)

Library of Congress Control Number: 2024945690

Faith is itself an act of resistance, a way of pushing back against the idea that the world is only as it appears to be. It is about the assertion of something in which everything is deeply connected, something that persists even in the face of despair.

—A. D.

Contents

Introduction: Navigating Faith in a Complex World. . . . ix

Chapter One: Technology as the Modern Tree of Knowledge
Resistance: Creating Sacred Space 1

Chapter Two: The Babylonian Captivity of the Mind: How Technology Is Rewiring Our Body and Spirit's Health
Resistance: Digital Detox, Weekly Digital Sabbath. . . 15

Chapter Three: God Dwelt Among Us: Embodiment
Resistance: Meditation 37

Chapter Four: All Bodies Are Prophets of Resistance
Resistance: Prayer 51

Chapter Five: The Temptation of Modern Spiritualism
Resistance: Gathering in Community 75

Chapter Six: Revitalizing Life Together: A Call to Kinship
Resistance: Communal Prayer and Sacramental Life 97

Chapter Seven: Faith in Action: Ruined for Life
Resistance: Social Justice and Environmental Activism 119

Chapter Eight: Unabashed Faith—Living an Authentic, Resilient, Christian Life
Resistance: Create a Rule of Life 151

Acknowledgments 165
Appendix: Questions of the Novice 167
Glossary 175
Bibliography 179
About the Author 191

Introduction

Navigating Faith in a Complex World

Creating a prayer life is essential, given the bombardment of digital distractions. The haptics of the phone must give way to devout, quiet moments that reconnect us to the living.
—A. D.

Developments in technology have progressed faster than ever in the last fifty years. I owned my first mobile phone thirty years ago and bought a PalmPilot (a device that kept your schedule) soon after. Schools were test-driving a new device called a tablet. A new moment was upon me and others like me. As first adapters, we were excited about the possibility of a more efficient organization and the opportunity to share our stories and faith. Soon enough came TheFacebook, as it was once called, Twitter, and Napster, which shared songs but ran into trouble because it evaded paying royalties to artists. Today, all of those tools and more are together in a device with more tech than the first lunar lander in 1969. However, along with other cultural trends, technology continued to expand while church attendance continued to decline.

Bowling Alone

Churches were not the only organizations in decline; so were fraternal orders, dance nights at the local private society, the Freemasons, bowling leagues, and the like. Where and how we gather began to reveal itself within the wider culture. Years ago, social scientist Robert Putnam wrote a book entitled *Bowling Alone* (2001). In it, he discusses the end of communal institutions such as bowling alleys, fraternal orders, and other places where people used to gather. He published a revised version of the book *Bowling Alone: The Collapse and Revival of American Community* (2020), suggesting the story was not over. For those curious about the shape of things in America, this became a modern classic in sociological and political science literature. It galvanized commentary and debate on the status of US society, both in academia and the world of policymaking. Bowling has been replaced with new digital forms of communication and connection. Humans have not stopped joining or gathering, but they do it less in real life.

While Putnam's analysis is dire, the conclusion is hopeful that the spirit of community in America can be rekindled by creating public places for people to gather, encouraging greater civic engagement for more people, building local communities, and enacting policies that support the family and community.

Throughout the last thirty years, the church has floundered with how to face the shifting cultural makeup of ever new and more diverse generations. It has been stumped in its search to find a solution that will take it back to the "glory days" and will shift the declining numbers. Of course, not all churches are declining. As a thirty-year student of the changes in society and within the church, I can see that, too. Many churches are thriving. This group of congregations is made up of various sizes. These churches share a core principle: their life together is one of authenticity. The second value is they have clarity regarding their unabashed faith. This is a faith that is neither hurtful to those seeking to rekindle life with God nor wishy-washy as to be hospitable while hiding their Christianity.

We are in a time of massive connectivity through technology that promises a new economy and opportunities to do good in the world. Yet, at the same time as this new technological connectivity is happening, we are becoming less connected to our families, our friends, and our wider communal life and responsibilities. We are closing in on ourselves and becoming lonelier and more disembodied. I hope to provide an answer for this loneliness and disconnection and share how a practice of unabashed faith can resist the anti-spiritual forces that seek to keep us at odds.

We are less connected to our humanity and the humanity of others, while a new mechanical age of spiritualism seems to make us sicker by the day. In and of themselves, human-created tools are not filled with good or evil; however, they may be used in such ways as to cause good and evil. The anti-spiritual forces that are the focus of this book are linked to the ancient heresy of dualism. Dualism, as this book will show, is marketed to us through the Internet and technology as a tree of knowledge, the focus on the disembodiment of the mind and spirit, the bodily harm inflicted by constant connectivity, the impacts upon energy use, racism, and economic justice. These are everyday forces that draw us from our created selves and undermine an unabashed faith.

Despite the ability to access unlimited amounts of data, we also become victims of misinformation and lack of wisdom. We can have anything delivered to our homes, but we miss out on the things that matter most—relationships with people who sell and serve in our communities. The desire to succeed and be popular has increased by its multiplication of likes beyond families and friend groups. Today, we aim to be influencers and stars for our social media followers and subscribers. We seek to manipulate our image so we no longer look like ourselves and then become fearful of people seeing us for who we are. We human beings, on the one hand, are paying for our time on social media through our commoditization by big corporations that are selling our interests and likes to the highest bidder.

On the other hand, we are attempting to sell our likes and dislikes to people we do not even know. This is a new way of thinking about economics and how money is made from human connections. I am not scaremongering here; the age of data and the tech economy are here to stay. I participate in it myself. This book will offer one answer to how we survive and become more human by doing so.

In real life, we have a bodily experience different from our online life. There are emerging studies that reveal how disconnected we feel. Nevertheless, the platforms insist that the promise is real, and we can be our best selves online. We understand that big tech mines our data and scrapes our profiles, thereby enabling better targeted marketing. Meanwhile, young adults hope for the moniker of influencer so they can turn followers into dollars.

I fully understand technology's future impact on new economies. Let me be clear: I do not fear technology and thus do not seek or suggest a pure life without it. You might be better for it, but I do not think we have a choice if we live in this world—we must be connected and help others connect. Things are changing, and we are waking up to many unhappy people, many of whom were left behind by the first wave of the tech revolution. Over 922 million people around the world are disconnected. Others are unhappy because the very language they speak is being left behind. Just as the psychological age brought new words into our vocabulary, technological advances and new tools are changing our vocabulary quickly.

Surveillance Capitalism

The frame of my lifetime began in the 1960s with a battery-powered transistor radio, electric trains, Easy-Bake ovens, three television stations, and power tools hooked up by electrical cords. It moved in the 1970s to battery-powered toy cars, walkie-talkies, and remote controls untethered from the machine. The first remote control for the TV had three buttons: power, forward, and backward. By the late 1970s, I was doing a math assignment that required programming a green box on a computer screen using code. At that exact moment, people in California were hooking massive computers together. In my life, I have moved from having parents who did not know where I was, to knowing exactly where my children and siblings are at all times through technology, if desired. We are quickly moving from constant connectivity through an age of a developing tech economy; we now find ourselves in a time that some describe as continuous surveillance, feeding capitalism. Now, we are shifting from a technological economy that amplifies and multiplies accessibility to one that becomes part of our workspace and bodies—we are becoming augmented (Zuboff, 2020).

Ghost in the Machine

The phrase *ghost in the machine* first appears in the work of the Oxford philosopher Gilbert Ryle in his 1949 book *The Concept of Mind*. It was a deliberate insult. Ryle used the phrase to attack René Descartes's theory of mind-body dualism. Cartesian dualism, as it is known, is the view that the mind and the body are two fundamentally different things and can be separated. The body, in this view, is corporeal, and it operates in the physical world. The mind (or soul, as is commonly meant by the use of the term), by contrast, is not of the body, and it exists independent of the body in an entirely separate realm, having some supernatural capacity to interact with the body.

Ryle maintained that this dualistic idea was fundamentally a mistake of categories, a basic logical error, because it treats the mind as a non-physical entity that somehow "lives inside" and directs the physical body, like a ghost that haunts a machine. He thought that this was illogical because it depended on the assumption that mental states (like thinking or feeling pain) were utterly unlike physical states (like moving or touching) rather than alternative modes describing the same things (Ryle, 1949).

Arthur Koestler then appropriated the phrase as the title of his book on philosophical psychology that today has a cult following: *The Ghost in the Machine* (1967). In it, Koestler engaged in vehement criticism of reductionist methodologies in philosophy, behaviorism, and other mechanicalistic approaches that seek to explain human experience and behavior within the context of machine processes. Think of it this way: he is against the theories proposed that people and animals learn and behave through their interactions with the environment and other creatures and, therefore, can be traced. This and similar theories assert that all behavior is learned through conditioning, which is a process of reward and punishment. Koestler's ghost in machine dichotomy promoted an intuitive approach to human experience, associating the specialness of the body's experience with spiritual and even transcendental properties. This is a kind of in-between theory that suggests there is always more going on than simply what is observed and, thus, we are creatures, not machines.

By coining the phrase *ghost in the machine*, both Ryle and Koestler sought to draw our attention to the limitations of thinking about the human mind–body composite in purely dualistic and mechanistic terms. Ryle's attack targeted the illogical nature of Cartesian dualism, while Koestler extended this critique to examine the fuller implications of paring back human experience to mere mechanics. The mind was not a machine, he argued (Koestler, 1967).

The musical artist Sting was reading a lot of Koestler in the 1980s. From his thinking about the theories presented in Koestler's books came the 1981 Police album entitled *Ghost in the Machine*. The album opens with "Spirits in the Material World." Then it continues with three songs amplifying the theme: "Too Much Information," "Rehumanize Yourself," and "One World (Not Three)." *Ghost in the Machine* then became an album that moved the ideas into popular music and framed the concerns of Koestler in musical terms. Sting, reflecting on the album and songs, talked about how a dualist approach was fodder for totalitarianism. He believed at the time that Koestler was holding up a mirror to the lives of the Northern Irish and other human conflicts around the world. Reflecting on his experience, Sting said in an interview:

> The reason we have to attack behaviorism is because it's been used by totalitarian regimes as an easy way of making people conform. A robot fits into big ideas much better. Whereas a thinking human being, a complex spiritual being, which is what we are, is out of place. You only have to look at the kids on the streets; they're becoming dehumanized (Sting, 1981).

Shortly after the album was released, there appeared a wholly separate yet interesting manga and anime series called *Ghost in the Shell* (1989–1990; 1995–1997). It depicted a near future in which humans start integrating themselves with machines. The stories take place in 2029 and follow a counterterrorism agency as they try to track down a cyber-criminal named the Puppeteer. This villain is a master of "ghost hacking." He performs crimes using the bodies of humans fitted with so-called cyberbrains. Spoiler: It turns out that the Puppeteer is an artificial intelligence that has taken up residence in a robot body. Masamune Shirow wrote the manga series. Production I.G. made an anime feature written and directed by Kenji Kamiyama. It aired from 2002 to 2005.

The anime film *Ghost in the Shell* (1995) is widely seen as an inspiration for the *Matrix* film series, which in turn borrowed specific elements, such as the dripping digital rain that the characters see, and the technique used to see inside the Matrix. Later, producer and director James Cameron cited *Ghost in the Shell* as one of his inspirations for *Avatar* (2009).

The Hard Problem

We have been examining a string of artistic conversations about the "ghost" and the "body." Each of these productions takes a slightly different angle of the story of mind–body dualism. The philosophical discussion has continued. In a book on consciousness entitled *The Character of Consciousness*, the philosopher David J. Chalmers coined the term *hard problem of consciousness* to refer to the problem of why and how mental phenomena or consciousness arise from physical activity in the brain. He calls this the "mind out there" (Chalmers, 2014).

In short, the "hard problem" is this: we know that the brain is made of neurons and that neurons send and receive information to and from each other in the form of electrical and chemical signals; but a thought, a condition of mind or feeling, or a mental picture of a sunset are something(s) of which we subjectively, as an individual, are aware of having an experience of—that is what people usually mean by "conscious." I am paraphrasing from my reading of Chalmers (2014). We know so much more today than ever before about how the brain works. We are close to knowing and understanding exactly how the neurons fire and are associated with behavior. However, what we do not know is why we have something called subjective experience. Chalmers is curious if we will ever know.

As one reads Chalmer's work, one begins to feel that perhaps there is, in fact, a type of ghost in the machine (at least in his theory). He is quick to add, though, that the mind is not something disconnected from the brain, but something extra created by it. Consciousness is not reduceable, Chalmers would argue, to a mere physical reality, but it is connected to it. Chalmers concludes, in almost all essays, with the notion that the question of how all this works is an intractable problem. Maybe it is even the *most* intractable in philosophy and cognitive science. I agree with Chalmers but want to be clear: I do not think consciousness can be separated from the body. It may surprise you to read that ancient theology holds tightly to this body, brain, and consciousness/spirit as one thing. This is such an essential concept in this book that it deserves a chapter of its own.

From Consciousness to Reason

Jonathan Haidt is a social psychologist. His work explains why science does not support such dualism. As I read his work, I became familiar with his thoughts on the body and reason. He is a researcher who can help us understand why we cannot jettison the body (Haidt, 2012). Haidt draws on various disciplines, including psychology, neuroscience, evolutionary biology, and anthropology, to argue that the mind is not separate from the body and instead is deeply interconnected with it. This means that consciousness and the notion of reason are a product of both brain and body.

Evolutionary psychology explains that human moral reasoning and emotions have developed over time to enhance survival and social cooperation. Haidt emphasizes the role of moral intuitions (automatic, visceral responses that guide moral judgment) arguing that these intuitions are deeply rooted in our evolutionary past and shaped by the body's sensory experiences.

Haidt frequently references neuroscience research to support this claim. The work of neuroscientist Antonio Damasio illustrates that emotions are fundamental to rational decision-making and moral reasoning. He suggests that bodily sensations play a connective role in decision-making by helping individuals evaluate options based on past emotional experiences (Damasio, 2008).

Haidt discusses the dual-process theory of cognition, distinguishing between two types of cognitive processes: intuitive (fast, automatic, and often emotionally driven) and reasoning (slow, deliberate, and logical). He argues that much of our moral thinking is dominated by intuitive processes rather than rational deliberation, reflecting a more embodied form of cognition. This agrees with the work of Nobel Prize winner Daniel Kahneman in his book *Thinking Fast and Slow* (Kahneman, 2011).

Haidt draws from the field of embodied cognition, which argues that cognitive processes are deeply rooted in the body's interactions with the world. He suggests that emotions and moral intuitions are not just "in the head" but are also experienced throughout the body, influenced by physical states and sensations. He incorporates anthropological findings that highlight the cultural and social-dimensional beginnings of morality, showing how different societies use rituals, bodily practices, and social norms to cultivate moral behaviors. For example, he discusses how practices like communal worship or shared meals foster a sense of belonging and moral cohesion, which he sees as grounded in bodily experiences and social emotions.

Haidt's work synthesizes various scientific resources to argue for an integrated view of the mind and body. He maintains that moral intuitions, emotions, and reasoning are not separate entities but rather are deeply interwoven with our bodily experiences and evolutionary heritage. This perspective challenges the Cartesian dualism that separates mind and body, emphasizing a holistic understanding of human psychology (Haidt, 2006, 2012).

The Body

We humans are language animals, and we are amazing creatures. We can think and reason and deliberate and discern. We can open ourselves up to creation and other people. We are curious. I find the work of theologians Charles Taylor, Rowan Williams, and David Bentley Hart on language interesting, and we shall touch on their work in later chapters. I also find Chalmers's theory of consciousness and its hard problem compelling. I also believe that there is something about our whole bodies that contributes to consciousness. For me, the body itself is necessary for consciousness.

The embodied cognition theory is an idea in psychology and cognitive science that challenges the traditional view that thinking and reasoning happen only in the brain or that this work can be separate from the body. Instead, this theory suggests that our thoughts, emotions, and decisions are deeply connected to our physical experiences in the world. It means that our body—including our senses, movements, and even our physical state—plays a crucial role in shaping our thoughts and feelings. This leads me to write about embodied prayer, thought, and action. My writing in this book will explore how our embodied experience leads to our embodied moral actions; how our emotional bodies play a role in our approach to the world and others; and how our physically embodied prayer changes our approach to other people; and, finally, how our language, and the spaces between the words, are authentic spaces that are felt by an awareness of the body.

The subject of this book, the core at the core, is a belief that our bodies matter, and that to say that something is "anti-spiritual" is to argue that it is *for* a dualistic approach to the mind and body, and *against* the fullness of what Christian theology offers in its wisdom of prayer and life.

Homo Deus—The Human God

In Yuval Harari's 2014 book *Sapiens: A Brief History of Humankind,* he argues that we are becoming a new form of humankind and that technology is changing us. In his follow-up book, *Homo Deus* (2017), he invites us to consider a future in which we could be a new species for whom information and data become a religion that serves the new human agenda of becoming. This is one trajectory for our future, and it is highly debated. The question he seeds is this: Are we becoming something different and less human because of our enmeshment with technology? We will explore Harari's ideas later in this book.

Embodied Community Evolution

Technology's impact goes beyond our mental and emotional health. It's reshaping our relationships, our communities, our global economy, and even our understanding of reality. Where the Church once stood as a cornerstone of communal life, we now engage and connect through screens rather than in sanctuaries. Church leaders hope people will use online worship to find a new spiritual home. This is a good choice for those who are homebound or unable to be physically present. This makes me revisit whether we are using the tech to help us grow closer together or further apart. This will be a question for future religious leaders as they ponder how they engage in their online relationships. This shift has profound consequences, not just for how we connect but also for how we experience the world itself. As humans journey into their digital lives, embodied lives can feel less real or less meaningful.

As I listen to my brothers, sisters, and siblings of younger generations, I hear their concerns regarding economic instability, mental health struggles, environmental crises, and the ethical challenges posed by artificial intelligence (AI) and automation. There is a kind of social media echo chamber that keeps us focused, in our tribes, on those anxieties that most trouble us. There are blogs and social media platforms that have created an economy by fomenting anxiety. They make money through our anxiety regarding those different than our own tribe. This book will teach you that you are not helpless and can resist the constant technological connectivity that awaits in your future.

Resistance

This book is for those trying to live a robust, sustained, and authentic life in this increasingly complex (and sometimes overwhelming) world. Perhaps you are an avid technology enthusiast. You tend to think that a substantial amount of good can be accomplished using new technologies. However, at times you sense that something has gone awry—that many of your attachments no longer feel as good as they once were, that something important may be lost. Maybe you have noticed that many of your most meaningful relationships are becoming more superficial, more mediated through screens. This book will address that experience.

Faith

This book will point the way toward insights and practices that can fortify your faith, make it more resilient and sustaining, and enable you to build the connections we seek—with God, others, and ourselves. If you are deeply anchored in your Christian faith and are wondering what additional insights might be gained by looking away from your smartphone reflection, this book will bear fruit for you, too. If you are rediscovering your Christian roots or discovering them for the first time, this book will address relevant challenges and help you find your place in a changing church that is grappling with some of these questions, or worse, hoping it will all disappear.

We will travel together through a wealth of theological and scriptural traditions from the history of Christianity. At their best, they distill the wisdom about reality, identity, and the community that God has created space for. We will see how the Bible approaches the questions of identity, community, and reality in ways that continue to be radically pertinent. Our roadmap will attempt to show how theology can draw together the ancient and the contemporary in an intentional effort to uncover and channel the wisdom of God so as to discern a balance between our bodies and virtual realities.

Running throughout the book is a note on the embodiment of our faith—that Christianity is an incarnational religion, a belief in flesh and blood. It speaks to the importance of the physicality of our lives, of living our faith in real relationships and communities. In this, the book is the opposite of the disembodied nature of life on the Internet, even if you are reading this on your tablet. At a time when we are increasingly distracted by the virtual and debased by our bodiless communication, this book will remind us of the importance of the individual body, embodied community, and physicality in our experience of the divine. It will remind us of the human being-ness that God has given us.

Unabashed Faith aims to be a clear call to remember God's divinity and our humanness—our embodied-ness. We are both diverse in many ways and also one human race. I want to take an honest look at, and pastorally and practically address how, technology and modern life are subtly eroding our spiritual practices and authentic relationships. This book calls us to reclaim the in-real-life spiritual practices essential to a vibrant, authentic Christian faith. It is about being honest and recognizing the seductive allure of technology while prioritizing the deeper, more lasting connections between human relationships and spiritual depth. Yet there can be value in online spiritual practices, which is why this book will maintain that these should supplement, rather than supplant, the embodied and communal practices that provide the foundation of our faith.

Each chapter will have an embodied practice to give you an idea of the steps you may take to rethink how you spend your time in the service of engaging with God and with people.

To begin this effort, I invite you to start now with a small amount of work. Print out your schedule from your device. Some of you may not have an electronic calendar, so I invite you to get out your paper calendar. Look at the last month and write down the time you spent with God privately, the time you spent with others in prayer, and the time you served others without a quid pro quo. There is no shame in doing this. I invite you to do this so that you can see and begin to think about how this book might help you to develop a practice of prayer and meditation further. This is the beginning of the resistance. This is the first step of becoming aware, and it will provide a foundation for attentiveness.

An Unabashed Faith

This is not another book that is meant to scare you about technology. I choose not to participate in such a dialogue. Technology is no more than a marvelous human-created tool meant to enrich humankind. All tools we use at their best make us better humans and better neighbors. I enjoy reading *Popular Science* and learning about technological innovations and gadgets. And I come from a long line of creatives who never say never. However, I am not going to deny that technology is messing with us. Consider the locus of power. Where there is power, its use may or may not build humanity up. Power can unite all or only some. Power can be used to separate us from each other and from God. How does an unabashed faith bring something new to the conversation? Amidst its pastoral care and practical advice, this book offers a theology. As a study of people and culture in modernity, it recognizes that there is a technological narrative that has its disciples. This book seeks to provide one path home to an embodied, resilient faith that is lucid enough for the present moment.

You might be skeptical. A spirit of skepticism is only natural; however, the reaction to skepticism should be neither a blank dismissal nor a deferential acquiescence. Instead, it should inspire a curious mind to ask: How shall we engage? How shall we engage the profound tradition of Christian spirituality in ways that do justice to its best insights while taking seriously the technological changes that have proven hard to avoid?

By the time you reach the last page of this book, you will understand the hold or potential hold anti-spiritual influences have on your life and why technology is impartial to your well-being. You will also understand how unabashed faith and prayer can be a powerful method of resistance.

Chapter One

Technology as the Modern Tree of Knowledge

Resistance: Creating Sacred Space

In our human embrace of technology, we have forgotten the depth of an embodied soul in favor of the tempting allure of instant knowledge. We have planted in every generation our own tree of knowledge. Once again, we risk trading our true humanity for a fleeting sense of perfection and control.

— A.D.

Searching for Answers

Rabbi Jonathan Sacks, may his memory be a blessing, wrote that the sin of the first humans in the Garden of Eden was disobedience. Having heard God's command to them, and despite having also seen this tree whose fruit they should not eat, they chose the fruit over the former command. They gained access to knowledge of good and evil, but it was derivative rather than primary. Theirs was an ethic of shame before an ethic of guilt. They valued appearances—whether they could meet other people's expectations of them—more than they valued their own consciences.

This is precisely what Rabbi Maimonides meant when he contrasted truth and falsehood with "things generally accepted" (Maimonides, 1204). A guilt-based ethic is about an inner voice that tells you as decisively, "This is right, that is wrong" as it does, "This is true, that is false." A shame-based ethic concerns social convention and what others expect or want from you (Sacks, 2023).

As humans who are hungry for knowledge, we thirst and seek without a thought to the ramifications. We are building new and more excellent frameworks for technology and artificial intelligence (AI). This is particularly true given that people often believe they are free from the responsibility of repercussions generations down the road because they cannot imagine it. Enter the shame of the past actions of our direct and indirect forebears. Despite the warning flares going off everywhere and the assault upon our bodies and lives by the new technological era we are creating for ourselves, we press on to consume the hype. What we are not doing, in the midst of the present moment, is listening to our bodies and ancient wisdom, as Rabbi Sacks points out so well (Sacks, 2023).

As spirituality is increasingly enmeshed with technology and the Internet, religious questioning is taking a new shape—and location. With attendance at churches, synagogues, and mosques waning, more people—especially young people—are taking their existential queries to the web. One in five American adults now says the Internet is a "very important" source of religious or spiritual knowledge, according to a 2014 survey of 3,217 people by the Pew Research Center. Younger people are more likely to go online for spiritual guidance than to rely on an actual spiritual mentor (Alper, 2023).

My own faith tradition teaches me that we will continue to eat the fruit of the tree that promises so much knowledge. We will, in fact, not only do this (as we have done in recorded history) but also build our own tree, not of God's making, and hope it will feed us even better. Search the web for anything vaguely related to spirituality, and you'll find lists and debates of the most profound sort. Many inquire about God; "Do you believe in God?" is among the most popular online debate topics. Others ask about death: "Is there life after death?" Many turn to the spirit: "Do you believe in ghosts?" And even more challenge the very systems that underpin so much of human meaning—those who want to know "What is the religious truth?" and "What is the difference between religion and spirituality?" On a secretive website for super-anonymous question-answering, called *Hubpages*, you get to the heart of our appetite to ask and answer spiritual questions. "Is it normal for a small white light to appear over me every time I pray?" "Why is it so hard for atheists to like deists?" "Do Protestants and Catholics worship the same God?" "What sets the suffering of the religious and spiritual apart?" and "What is your religion?" "Why does religion exist?" And one last spiritual query: "What does Jesus want me to do now?"

I was asked the other day if we can expect a Jesus chatbot. I said, "Yes, because we are human." Who could have imagined people taking up personalities on social media and answering based on their character? We already have Jesus on Twitter (now called X). At the Burning Man festival, where people co-create a global ecosystem in the middle of the Black Rock desert, you can pick up a telephone receiver in a phone booth and speak to God; someone has signed up to be the voice of God on the other end.

The global thirst for meaning and purpose is remarkable. Anonymity on the Internet allows personal and often exposing questions to be explored. Yet this anonymity reflects the flattening out of spiritual engagement, where we browse and click "like," but rarely tackle the more profound question of, "What is my purpose here?"

This trend is further corroborated by findings from Google Search Trends, which indicate marked spikes in searches for those feeling drawn toward practices with a spiritual dimension, especially in times of global crisis—such as during the COVID-19 pandemic, when search terms such as *prayer, meditation,* and *Bible study,* spiked. This points to an increasing appetite for spiritual answers to searching questions in a world where many traditional compasses of meaning don't feel as accessible or reliable. Other examples from Google Trends reveal that people search for magical arts, healing, spirits, and divination (all Google Search Trends, various years).

Unfortunately, the spiritual bounty of the Internet has side effects. According to a 2020 "Rewired Soul Survey" report by the Barna Group on the state of the church in America, many lapsed churchgoers still expressed eager engagement with spirituality, and most of those seekers were spending their time on podcasts, YouTube, and social media. When we translate these tendencies into actual numbers, we discover that, despite its abundance, nearly 60 percent of respondents who went online to find spiritual content said they felt it was unhelpful or confusing. This juxtaposition of unprecedented abundance and ultimate lack—a spirituality without satisfaction—is the divine value of the Internet, which is as intuitively longed for as it is patently unwieldy (Barna Group, 2023).

These findings are further highlighted by research from the Oxford Internet Institute. Their 2019 study on religion online shows that the Internet has become a central space for those who call themselves spiritual but not religious and features a variety of content, from traditional religious forms to new-age practices. While the Internet has expanded individual access to spiritual information, what the Oxford study called a "spiritual smorgasbord" can lead to fragmentation as seekers struggle to make sense of the diverse content and to find coherent and satisfactory forms of spiritual learning (Oxford Internet Institute, 2019).

These works above collectively make clear the intimate, kaleidoscopic nature of digital spirituality—a space in which the hunger for meaning is no less visceral than its fractures. The Internet's cognitive ecology implicates itself with a detached, pluralistic spiritual existence no longer connected to the wisdom of the ancients or the traditions of centuries. At times, it takes you out of your frame of mind rooted in the body. This search affects the human body—of that, there is no doubt.

The Embodiment of Worship

Unless worship engages the senses—sight, sound, touch, taste, and smell—it fails at anchoring faith in the body. The body and the community are not just additions to the worship experience; they are integral to the nature of the experience. It is in the totality of the practice that the divine encounter is experienced. The poor translation of that experience into digital worship is one of distortion. While digital worship can carry information and allow for some forms of connection, it cannot fully replicate the sensory richness of in-person worship. The preceding research tells us that there is sensory impoverishment going on. Such impoverishment leads to disembodied worship experiences that feel incomplete.

Does this mean that people who gather, pray, and worship online are not having a spiritual experience? No. There is, though, an aesthetic quality of difference between the two that is important as part of the continued act of co-creation with God that is unmediated through technology.

The essence of Christian spirituality is communal, and, as an extension of this, the shared physical presence of the body is vital to being a community in the total sense. The Church as the Body of Christ is most fully itself, and the community most fully experiences and enacts its corporate identity, when it is gathered physically together. This is not just about being in the same place; it's about "enacting" the life of the Church together through the physical, embodied act of gathering. Of course, virtual gatherings can be worthwhile. However, these should not be seen as competing with in-person gatherings. Virtual gatherings, as indispensable as they were during the pandemic, are in no way a replacement for the distinctive spiritual and corporate life experienced by believers when they gather physically.

There are differences between making sacred space and digital space. When Christians gather to worship God, they tend to do it in a holy space or make the space in which they gather physically sacred. Worship takes place in a holy physical space, generally just another term for a church, chapel, cathedral, or other building intended for prayer, often consecrated for that purpose. Today, Christians gather and make space outside the church sacred by undertaking sacred acts in the world.

Sacred Space Is the Wild

Here is the ancient image for all Abrahamic faiths: Abraham and Sarah leaving the land of Ur and, as they go, setting up altars in the wilderness for God. For all practical purposes, space within the created world is God's and worthy of being marked by sacred acts. Wherever liturgy and worship take place, the physical space is sacramentally charged. The integral nature of physicality in spaces made sacred makes it possible to argue that the digital is only ever temporary and supplementary.

Given the role that embodiment and materiality play in the worship experience, Christians and Christian leaders should consider carefully maintaining the elements of physicality among worshippers. While online forms of church will continue to emerge in the coming years, it is only through the physical presence, the sensuality, the faithful community, and the space of worship that a Christian spirituality remains animated. Without all these things, the practice of faith becomes more a matter of individual taste as opposed to being decidedly and distinctively Christian.

Your Wild Sacred Space

Humans have been practicing setting apart space for sacred bodily work for most of recorded time. The Abrahamic faiths, the Asian–Pacific religions, African religions, Bronze Age peoples, and Indigenous peoples have created sacred spaces. Sanctifying spaces within the home and designated places of worship as sacred spaces where digital devices are not welcome and where one can disconnect is the first step toward cultivating a resistance practice in your life.

Over thousands of years, people have created sacred spaces where they spend their lives as a reminder that they are surrounded by the sacred. In the same way that Abraham and Sara built altars in the wilderness where God was found, you are invited to do the same. We are invited to choose to live in a world of aestheticism, a world of beauty.

Aesthetics is not just about visual, aural, and tactile appeal—it expresses purpose, intentionality, and meaning. It speaks to a larger world of possibilities than the brittle, mechanistic worlds in which technology is often conceived. In this setting, this space you will carve out speaks to the possibility of life beyond yourself to the divine and others.

Aesthetics radically differs from the perspectives that dominate much of our contemporary style—the mechanical function and taste perspectives. The mechanical model hopes to narrow in on the components or parts of a complex system and reduce them to their purportedly fundamental physical reality. Aesthetics emphasizes the whole, where the whole is greater than the sum of its parts.

The difference between "aesthetics" and taste can be thought of as the difference between experience and reality. Taste is a subjective response to an objective phenomenon, like the experience of engaging with beauty and art. How one might judge and value form, style, expression, etc., depends upon cultural, psychological, and individual factors. Taste, by its very nature, is always finite—a particular response to art, to nature, and so on, at a given place and a given time; it is historically limited and, perhaps to some degree, socially limited as well. It is the expression of an ideologically conditioned will.

Instead, "aesthetics" refers to an objective reality that points to a higher, indeed transcendent, divine order of being. Seen this way, "aesthetics" refers not to simple matters of individual or collective taste but to a fundamental character of reality that reflects the beautiful, an emanation from the divine. It points outward, beyond the subjective, to a reality that exists independent of human perception and cultural construction, a transcendental truth that reveals something real, indeed fundamental, about the nature of God and creation.

An unabashed faith understands that aesthetics and beauty exist without my presence being required. It is a recognition that God is wholly other than I am and not dependent upon my existence or my taste.

This space I am describing is a space to open yourself up, a place to breathe, a place of peace. This space is more significant than any artifacts that appeal to your senses that you may put there. This is a space where you may build a particular type of experience that is making something fruitful or fructifying for the human spirit and doing so by attending to the human condition through God's beauty and the beauty of the body and creation.

Creating a sacred space at home for the practice of prayer, meditation, and solitude is an intensely personal activity that could transform your home and your spiritual life. By demarcating space for silence and meditation, you create a "house of prayer"—where you can retreat from the hustle and bustle of everyday digital life and engage in a profound and intimate dialogue between your body and God. Here are some tips on creating a home meditation space for yourself where you can find quiet to be alone or walk in mindfulness.

Resistance Recap: Choose a Quiet Corner

Find a quiet space with low foot traffic where you will not be disturbed. It can be a small area in a living room. It may be in a bedroom or a carved-out space in another room. The important thing is finding a space to which you can return consistently. This is where you will practice being offline. You can inhabit the space together if you have a partner or spouse, sharing or taking turns. I had a monk once tell me that one of the things we need is to practice doing one thing at a time. This is the space for practicing one thing.

This choice of place shapes the association that forms over years of experience. This is the constancy of space made holy by prayer. When I sit, the space around me becomes a bodily cue that it is time to withdraw my attention from the outer world and turn it inward.

Clear the Space

Clear the space of clutter and distractions. It should be clean and sparse, free from things that distract the mind, so that the body can relax. It is a no-phone, no-tech, no-TV area. Keep the decoration basic and straightforward, with minimal furniture. Or, if you are a person who loves art, fill the walls with sacred art. I believe sparse is the best; however, if you choose to bring things into the space, they should redirect you back to the work of prayer, meditation, and contemplation. For years, I did not have space like this, so I did the best I could, and I added things into the space that would help me return to my prayer.

A space without clutter is a body without clutter. Clean up the physical environment so that the "busyness" of sights can drop and allow the mind to settle. This is what sacred space in a sanctuary is about. There are things in a sanctuary that are meant to draw you to God and other people. Our bodies remember space, and routine use helps all the senses quiet.

Comfortable Seating

Some people like to sit in a chair. I am a comfortable soft chair guy. You can also take a comfy cushion and a recognizable seat—perhaps a mat—so you can sit upright for long periods on the floor. You can sit cross-legged on the floor with your back tall. However, if you sit in a chair, your sense of sitting must be at ease in that specific position. Regardless of which way you decide, it is essential that it be comfortable for your body.

People will say you need to do yoga and sitting meditation; maybe you do, but that is not for everyone. There are many body types; do not let this part of the preparation be frustrating. Everyone can find a place they love, and I genuinely believe that every human body can find a comfortable position for prayer and meditation.

Lighting and Ambiance

Use soft lighting to create a soothing sanctuary space. You might add some candles, a lampshade with a warm golden glow, or let the light dance in through a window. Make it as bright or as dim as you like. This is a personal choice. What I am suggesting, though, is that it can be sunlight in the early morning to candlelight or sunset light. The critical thing to remember is that your meditation environment will influence your bodily state. The ambiance and light should signal to the body that something different happens here.

You can add to this space as you want. Some people live in loud, noisy places and find music helps create a reflective mood. A good meditation skill, though, will allow you to meditate anywhere with whatever sounds are around you. But we will get to practice later. For now, make your environment a space that signals sacredness. If you, like many, invite a priest to come and bless your home or you do so during the season after Christmas, then you might do so with a particular intention for this space.

Some people can do this; for others, home may be too busy with too many distractions. God is not only present when you make sacred space for God. God is present everywhere, so I invite you to move out of your idea that this space has to be in a home and think more broadly about your day and routines.

There are two ways of thinking about sacred space; the first is a space you visit in your home. The second can be the reclamation of sacred space anywhere in the world where you are. Perhaps you work near a church or sanctuary of some kind. If open, you can go there before work, at lunch, or even after work before you go home. Finding open sanctuaries for you to use is a great practice. In big cities, this is recognizably easier than in smaller towns. Nevertheless, being able to find such spaces is just another resource. You might try to find one that works and use it regularly.

Additionally, you can include more than sanctuaries or homes. Think about outside your home, your garden, a park near you, or a particular kind of walk through a specific neighborhood that you can return to regularly. I am suggesting a spiritual practice of designating space(s) where you can touch the divine and be touched by the divine. So, find a retreat space in your neighborhood. Find a bench, peer into a quiet street, drop into a small, secret garden, a big tree to sit under, or venture into less populated parts of your town or city. Any of these can be a peaceful spot you can use as a sacred space the next time you need a few moments alone.

Our Space Has Meaning

This sacred chosen space, not just the objects in it, has meaning. I suggest that there is a being-ness (an ontology) to the space itself. Through a reading of visual art theory, I suggest that things are not only what is inside or outside but also the space in and around them.

Here, we begin to approach space differently by considering what lies in between objects.

Silence in prayer signifies a critical gap, an absence that is substantive, now present between objects. It is within these spaces, between objects, that communication emerges. These gaps are as significant as a word, an object, or a sound. The theatricality of the metaphor itself and the in-betweenness is crucial in revealing the relationships of things. In other words, our awareness of communication and nature can only manifest if there is silence between God and ourselves, ourselves and others.

As technology encroaches on our lives more and more, it is imperative that we find ways to resist. One of the ways we can do this is by curating our sacred space to help us find places of rest and peace.

Chapter Two

The Babylonian Captivity of the Mind: How Technology Is Rewiring Our Body and Spirit's Health

Resistance: Digital Detox, Weekly Digital Sabbath

We are handing over our bodies into the electronic arms of digital gods in their mythic worlds. We are ensnared by addiction into a digitally connected hell, a figurative Babylon, with ourselves.
— A. D.

There are profound bodily implications stemming from the permeating nature of technology in our lives. I use the "body" because we are not minds alone, but rather a body with a mind, nervous and gastrointestinal systems, biological organisms, and a soul, or you may call it spirit. As human beings, we are a living body filled with living bodies in both the spiritual and physical sense. We are increasingly connected to a non-real technological space that plays with our body as it encounters it. We need to recognize that there is some difference in how all people curate their online experiences. Research helps us understand but cannot fully describe everyone's experience. Technology challenges our bodies. Being plugged in all the time sets the stage for anxiety, depression, and attention issues. Additionally, biases in the digital frameworks further amplify these challenges, especially for marginalized communities. As a result, we are in a moment I refer to as the Babylonian Captivity of the Mind.

The Babylonian Captivity of the Mind

The Babylonian Captivity refers to the suffering of people in ancient Israel at the hands of the Babylonians and as a metaphor for suffering people throughout the ages. The cultural identity of the people of Israel has always been a bodily connection to their homeland, just like the Palestinians, and people from all over the world claim their own geographical context. Sometime in the sixth century BCE (Before the Common Era), Babylon (located in current-day Iraq) sacked Israel. Through a forced migration to Babylon, many Israelites found themselves in a land they did not know. That land was filled with other gods. The life they knew and the ways they worshiped had ended with the razing of the Temple in Israel.

The prophets named Ezekiel and Isaiah spoke to the people. They were honest with them. They told the people that they had forgotten others. They had forgotten God in their livelihood, and they had forgotten to care for neighbors, widows, orphans, and the hungry. They had become so wrapped up in their own lives that perhaps they thought they had become the center of the world—and that was spiritually unhealthy for them. This is a powerful story within both Christianity and Judaism.

We cannot consider the oppression of others to be equal to our current burden; yet, there is something to our moment that is becoming a captivity. We are learning to worship new gods and paying more attention to feeding technology and its manipulations than one another. Are we on a genuine, global, forced migration into a new world not of God's creation but of our own pretend mastery?

Isaiah told the people, in the book by the same name, Isaiah 59:1, "Behold, the Lord's hand is not shortened, that it cannot save; nor his ear heavy, that it cannot hear." Someday, the nations would see God's salvation. Isaiah predicted a day when "every valley shall be exalted, and every mountain and hill made low" (Isaiah 40:4). In this emerging age, I want you to know that God is love and that God's love. Connection to that love can change your life, especially if you feel underwater in this "Internet of Things," as some technologists call it. (For more about the Internet of Things, or IoT, see the glossary.)

God's love will indeed ask you to change your body's position. Quite literally, I refer to *metanoia,* which is an ancient Greek word for changing direction. The work of this book is going to ask you to change direction.

Shoshona Zuboff illustrates in her book, *The Age of Surveillance Capitalism,* that we are dealing with more than captivity by digital omnipresence and continued connectivity. Her in-depth connections reveal that our captivity is linked to wealth and power that are scraping and mining the data that we freely upload (Zuboff, 2020). In my tradition, we call powers and principalities those in this world that seek to corrupt and destroy the creatures of God. While in captivity, our data, emotions, likes, and dislikes are being used to target us and our families, and then the information is sold to advertisers.

William Stringfellow was an American lay theologian, lawyer, and social activist whose work has dramatically influenced twentieth-century Christian theologians like Karl Barth, and vice *versa*. Stringfellow was an Episcopalian and served as a prophetic voice to the American Church and culture, constantly struggling with the intersections of faith, politics, and social life. A central moral theme in his writings is how "the Powers"—the institutions, systems, and ideologies that help to constitute human life and society—tend to become sources of domination and dehumanization, contrary to the life-affirming message of the Gospel.

In *An Ethic for Christians and Other Aliens in a Strange Land*, Stringfellow explained the notion of "Babylon" as a metaphor for the all-pervasive influence of the powers in daily life: "The Bible story of the Babylonian Captivity has to do with aliens who did not expect it, however, and had to learn a strange language. . . . Exiles are the experience of Christians throughout the millennia" (Stringfellow, 1973, 59). "The Powers appeal to us right here and now," he added. So, it becomes the vocation of the people of God, following the example of Jesus, "to live permanently as aliens in a world pervaded by 'Babylon'—even where it is concealed in a religious flash-bulb pretending to be Christianity" (ibid.). For Stringfellow, Babylon is not only a vanished empire of yore; it represents any society or culture that oppresses, degrades, and dehumanizes people (Stringfellow, 1973). Some of these themes influenced my book *Citizen* and the notion of dual citizenship.

These powers become the main focus of Stringfellow's *Conscience and Obedience* (1977). In this book, Stringfellow delves into how Christians are to respond to political powers and systems that are hostile to the faith. He critiques the most familiar verse for asserting obedience to political authorities of all kinds: Romans 13:1–7. He contrasts it to what amounts to the most subversive verse in scripture, Revelation 13:10: "He that leadeth into captivity shall go into captivity: he that killeth with the sword must be killed with the sword. Here is the patience and the faith of the saints." The two quotes together reveal the essence of radical political conscience that is our destiny: "If Caesar says, 'Be still,' and the risen Jesus says, 'Preach the gospel,' whom are you going to obey?" (Romans 13:1–7). The powers are idolatrous; therefore, Christians must resist and subvert and are called by an unabashed faith to pledge absolute and faithful allegiance to Christ.

When read today, William Stringfellow casts a strong and unwavering critique of modern life that calls Christians everywhere to recognize and resist the ways institutions continue to make us cogs in ever-new machinery—a part of a timeless movement to dominate and control people and the planet. His work remains urgent and alive for anyone who wants to speak to people's questions about the spiritual aspects of social justice and the role of faith in struggling with the tensions of modernity. The tool of technology has made us a cog in the wheel that benefits the powers and principalities of this world. We live in captivity.

Prophets: The Mental Health Impacts of Constant Connectivity

Let us begin with a symphony of voices heralding the people's suffering and crying in our time. Research is a form of listening. We aggregate it, and it can help us understand things in the world around us. Peer-reviewed research may not necessarily fit your personal experience, but that does not mean the research is faulty. Instead, when you discover that research is out of tune with your life, it more likely means that you are not part of the aggregate sampling and have more in common with outliers who were part of the research. In my tradition as an Episcopalian, we are not afraid of science or research. We are not biblical literalists. So, research is an integral part of listening to the world—it is essential. The concerns I am about to share are those echoed in my weekly bishop visits with people. I listen to relatives, friends, young adults, and children, all echoing the research in this book. I hear the same concerns from other clergy, and I hear this from educators. Many of us are saying the same thing—we are suffering. Perhaps you are suffering and that is why you picked up this book in the first place, so you can get some help with what ails you—that which is working against a spirituality of wellness and connectedness.

Research has revealed that too much digital connectedness increases stress, anxiety, and depression in our bodies; this is probably not news to you. The American Psychological Association (APA) found in 2017 that "constant checkers"—those who check their digital devices frequently—report much higher stress levels than those who take breaks from their devices. The APA says that we have lost the cadence of daily living and that constant digital connection can lead to chronic stress and burnout (APA, 2017).

A study published by the University of Gothenburg in Sweden concluded that excessive smartphone use—especially before bedtime—adversely affects sleep quality and is associated with increased anxiety and depression (Harenstam, 2015). The study concluded that reducing screen exposure may relieve psychological distress.

Our tendency to use digital media when we should be engaging in more profound, more purposeful activities has also been well documented. Research demonstrates that personal mobile devices can fragment attention and undermine many forms of prolonged, absorbent, and contemplative activity—whether sacred or secular—from prayer and meditation to a combination of reading and writing.

A 2014 study at the University of California, Irvine, by Gloria Mark, also published in the *New York Times*, found that constant interruptive use of digital technology reduces attention span, focusing abilities, and depth of thought (Mark, 2014). This disjointed attention becomes the norm, even when turned inward, as in contemplation. Consider that the first mobile phone with a capacitive touchscreen was the LG Prada, released in May 2007 just before the iPhone, so the 2014 data is very early in our phone and screen use research.

Nicholas Carr wrote *The Shallows: What the Internet Is Doing to Our Brains*. In it, he describes how the Internet promotes a type of distracted skimming, clicking, and quitting that characterizes the way we read online and is evident in other research as well. We are rewiring our brains, he suggests, and this will not help us to read books or long pieces of writing. It is antithetical to the sustained, deep attention required for fruitful spiritual practice (Carr, 2011).

A 2018 poll from the Pew Research Center reported that 60 percent of US adults described their digital devices as a significant distraction from their most important activity (one of those being their spiritual lives), while only 39 percent stated the same about TV, books and magazines, movies, and music (Pew Research Center, 2018). This data spotlights the breadth of the problem, as many people report that controlling their attention away from digital interruption in the service of spiritual life is a challenge for them. We are being formed by tech and gadget usage. The findings suggest that if we are honest, we value devices more today than "in real life" (IRL) experiences. These devices are a distraction, and we allow them to be so.

Physical and Physiological Effects of Digital Distraction

The body is affected. This is not merely an effect upon the eye or mind but our whole physical and physiological body. Digital distraction thus hinders spiritual practices because they are rooted in the physical and physiological as well. Anxiety, lack of sleep, and the level of distractedness affects your ability to quiet yourself. As your body accepts the frenetic pace of distraction, you are less able to do the very thing that would help the body calm. Our bodies are not meant to run in the frenzied way created by constant connectivity. Studies indicate that online synchronous digital media use shares characteristics with addiction (Burén et al., 2023). The research is quite convincing.

The most recent literature on the effects of this permanent digital life has focused on how various factors of mobile device usage—how much, which content, when (especially after dark), which kind of media, and how many devices—seem to determine the extent of the self-reported health effects of the screen time, ranging from poor sleep quality and increased risk for cardiovascular disease to high blood pressure, weight gain, and low HDL, thus correlating to stress regulation and insulin resistance (Lissak, 2018).

From a psychological perspective, higher screen times are interconnected with both internalizing—which refers to a range of mental health issues linked to anxiety, fear, sadness, and the overall negative evaluation of self-worth—and externalizing, which refers to a range of aggressive, impulsive, or antisocial behaviors often related to one's actions. Again, in both sets of issues, trouble with sleep seems to be an underlying factor. Research has linked symptoms of depression and even suicidality to screen-related disruptions to sleep, use of digital devices at night, and phone dependency.

Psychoneurological research confirms that excessive screen use diminishes social coping abilities and induces craving behaviors similar to those caused by drug addiction. Alterations in regions that affect cognitive control and emotional regulation in the brain have been repeatedly implicated in digital media addiction. A case study of a nine-year-old boy with an ADHD diagnosis saw a significant reduction in behaviors associated with his symptoms after cutting down screen time, which may suggest that ADHD diagnoses may sometimes result from screen time-induced behaviors. Given the available evidence, it is clear that we need to do much more research to identify the tangible role of digital media as a factor influencing the balance between mental and physical health (Lissak, 2018).

A Harvard Medical School study found that the impact of blue light from screens alone reduces melatonin production, the quality of one's sleep, and, by extension, cognitive function through to the next day—thus also impacting one's ability to focus in prayer or meditation. Conversely, some research indicates that pre-sleep interventions, such as prayer, meditation, or scripture reading, improve sleep and mood, peace, and wellness (*Harvard Health*, 2024).

Algorithmic Bias and Discrimination

Constant connectivity might have psychological effects that differ from user to user. Still, systemic disadvantages begin to deepen psychological burdens when algorithmic biases amplify historical inequities of marginalized communities by embedding the bias in digital platforms. Consider the quantitative study of Safiya Umoja Noble. In her book *Algorithms of Oppression: How Search Engines Reinforce Racism* (2018), she describes how search engines often reify abstract institutional systems of racism and sexism by displaying consistent sets of biased results to queries. This is because the absence of diversity among those who create the algorithms often leads to the propagation of harmful stereotypes. Searches for Black women or girls, for example, frequently produce derogatory content that objectifies Black women, demonstrating the entrenchment of racial and gender biases within these digital architectures.

The *AI Now Institute Report* released ahead of the first Conference for Fighting Racist AI notes that using artificial intelligence systems in societal decision-making processes will likely reinforce racial and gender biases. It is argued in that report that the tech industry (which preponderantly consists of white and Asian men) creates AI systems that do not necessarily consider the experiences and requirements of minorities. An interesting article looked at AI-generated images of autistic people and is a good short piece on the point of this section. All the pictures were of white, thin, young men (Crimmins, 2023). This absence of relevant data regarding people of color in AI systems will result in algorithms more welcoming to equality violations, notably in criminal justice, recruitment, and lending (AI Now Institute, 2019).

Lack of Diversity in Tech Leadership and Development

Let us go deeper. A lack of representation within tech development is a clear contributor to the preservation of systemic biases online, which ultimately affects psychological and social outcomes in marginalized communities.

The Kapor Center, a group of committed individuals working toward a just technological ecosystem, published the *Tech Leavers Study* in which they state: "Of all workers, women and people of color are underrepresented in tech jobs, especially in leadership." The report continues to state that of people who left the tech industry, 78 percent said they had been mistreated, and women and people of color were likelier to say so. Lack of diversity at the leadership and decision-making level means that the voices of women and people of color are put further from the creation of the digital tools we use—tools that are already seeding these biases, further striating American society (Kapor Center, 2017)

McKinsey & Company, one of the largest consulting firms in the world and the leader in management consulting, published a diversity report entitled *McKinsey & Company's Diversity Wins Report,* which found that companies with executive teams of more diverse genders and ethnicities generally have better outcomes across a variety of technological fields than their peers. For instance, the research found that tech companies with less diverse leadership teams are likely to "produce services that do not serve the needs and experiences of diverse users—from teens to older adults of all ethnicities," leading to "biased outcomes, possibly exacerbating discriminatory issues like racism and xenophobia" (McKinsey & Company, 2020).

Online Harassment and Xenophobia

The result of algorithmic bias is a psychological toll that is exacerbated by always-on behaviors, which then multiply the high rates of online harassment of those marginalized by hate groups. Therefore, exposure vulnerability through design and moderation reflects a lack of meaningful diversity in the platform creation and stewardship. The Pew Research Center reports in "Online Harassment: Marginalized People" that this is particularly true for racial minorities and those who fall under the LGBTQ+ umbrella, who are more likely to face severe forms of harassment online, namely physical threats, sustained harassment, and cyberstalking, than their white heterosexual and male counterparts (Vogels, 2021; see also Matamoros-Montgomery and Farkas, 2021). This suggests that to protect more people's bodies, website owners, digital developers, and algorithm designers must be held responsible for platforms that harbor and protect people who undertake these behaviors. Why? Because we are not made up of feelings or minds alone; we are a system of a whole body. This is not just how we may feel; we are participating in psychological and physiological damage to one another.

The Digital Divide and Its Impact on Marginalized Communities

The gap between groups within society that have or do not have access to digital technologies is called the digital divide. The digital divide exposes how having access to the Internet and having digital literacy is more challenging for marginalized communities, further entrenching social inequalities (Kaufmann, 2024). For example, in the absence of an internet connection, these communities would be excluded from taking part in the digital economy as well as from the creation of platforms, which might lead to a lack of diverse voices in the conception of digital frameworks and inclusion of social biases concerning in-person communities. This divide was highlighted during COVID-19 when schools and businesses went online and remote, thus alienating students regarding curriculum and teacher access, and workers could not access their workplace

(Annie E. Casey Foundation, 2024). You can check out the Internet Poverty Index here: https://worlddata.io/portfolio/internet-poverty-index.

Implications for Mental and Spiritual Well-being

The data suggests that this lack of diversity in the development and leadership of tech impacts what gets created and heavily influences the perpetuation of systemic biases online, such as racism, xenophobia, and other targeted forms of bias. This bias creates digital frameworks that keep communication spaces unsafe for many. Moreover, when our bodies must operate within marginalized frameworks that are stressful or hostile systems, our health suffers the effects. This could manifest in increased anxiety or depression and reinforces a cycle of disconnection.

We know that constant connectivity, regardless of who we are, is changing us. It is making us more anxious, angry, and depressed. Our bodies are suffering the effects of anti-spiritual forces that we are addicted to and will be required to operate within the coming technological economy. We have ventured to eat of the tree of knowledge without considering the cost.

Spiritual Distraction

I know many tech workers. Nearly one third of the workforce in the West works remotely now. Tech workers are creative, brilliant, and excited about the future. The tech workers I know want to do good. They want to help provide the new connective roots of the world in which we will exist. This is the reality of our new economy, and we will all be living within some form of it.

Be that as it may, technology as it stands today is an assault on the dignity of human beings. We are doing it to ourselves. I am sitting here writing on a laptop with my tablet connected as a separate screen, surfing the net for data to help me, with my phone to my right, watching every moment for new texts. I have not checked email or social media more often today because of my commitment to finish this book. We are all involved. It is the fruit we are consuming for all kinds of reasons. As someone who cares for people, I am saying this is not good for us. Our bodies are suffering.

My next book, with the working title "Beyond Code and Creed," will examine a new way of thinking about ethics in the technological age. For now, we must name what is happening and how we are being captivated and becoming economically and bodily arrested by gods of our own making.

The maddening pace of the informational environment and the compulsive velocity of digital contact constitute essential, yet sometimes hidden, challenges to the life of the spirit, if not outright destructive forces, as investigated earlier.

Theological Insights on Resistance

This situation of distracted attention isn't new, but the challenge of maintaining spiritual attention in an age of digital acceleration and omnipresence is more significant than ever. The writings of such theological observers as Thomas Merton and Simone Weil speak volumes about the spiritual importance of attention.

When I first began to learn the art of contemplative prayer and meditation, my teacher sent me to the book *The Cloud of Unknowing* (anonymous) and the writings of Thomas Merton. Merton stressed the importance of silence and solitude as keys for spiritual growth: "Our life is hidden, but our life is busy. . . . We must get rid of our noise to touch our hidden life" (Merton, 1986). In this light, we can better understand how digital noise disrupts the silence in which true contemplation and prayer can occur.

Simone Weil, French philosopher, mystic, and political activist (raised in a Jewish home; she would later say that she felt more at home in the Christian imagination), speaks of similar themes. There is no question that Weil, like Merton, was a mystic. She also points to the central role of attention in all things spiritual: "Attention, taken to its highest degree, is the small secret of all spiritual greatness," she once said. "Attention is the rarest and purest form of generosity." In a world of relentless digital distraction, the ability to give one's full attention—to God, to others, to oneself—becomes ever more complicated but becomes even more crucial for spiritual health. This was first published in 1951 in *Waiting for God* (Weil, 1979).

Reclaiming Attention for Spiritual Depth

While it may feel overwhelming to contend with the anti-spiritual influences in your life, especially those in a life of constant connectivity, your body can become a means of resistance. In my tradition, we have ancient practices, just as in other traditions, that involve the body and offer a spiritual form of resistance and a valuable antidote to the fractured experience of digital living.

Bodily commitments of sitting, kneeling, standing, singing, praying, and listening are ways we orient our bodies to God and others in prayer. The sacramental life of the Episcopal Church, and maybe your own, is positioned to the body (with its wholeness of soul, mind, biological life, and living organisms) and oriented to God. It is a form of bodily practice. It is a practice that takes time and requires effort and learning as you do it. Unlike many other parts of our lives, there is no shame in learning and failing in such practices. At the very core, it is coming to terms with the fact that life is quite unmanageable and that there is something greater outside of you that can help: "A power greater than yourself," say my friends in Alcoholics Anonymous, a program deeply influenced by my tradition. That brings us back to the body and helps orient us to a more whole and meaningful life of spiritual practice. In a world increasingly dominated by digital interactions, this kind of practice becomes vitally important.

In an era of pervasive digital distractions, reclaiming the body's capacity for attentiveness and stillness is essential for cultivating deep spiritual practices. The digital age, characterized by constant connectivity and information overload, fragments our focus and makes engaging in sustained spiritual reflection challenging. I believe with all my heart that these embodied practices refocus our whole selves and our whole bodies on God, offering practical recommendations and personal reflections to help individuals deepen their spiritual lives amidst the distractions of the modern world.

Embodied practices, such as prayer, meditation, and participation in the liturgy, help restore attention and recover a reunified focus upon the divine. We are not just minds plugged into the machine. Embodiment trains and holds the body's attention and helps us achieve a greater spiritual level of reality by becoming present.

Physical bodily actions deploy the body's senses when we practice them alone or with others. These are not symbolic actions at their best; they are, in fact, rituals. Moreover, it is important to recognize that this bodily ritual of reorientation is itself disruptive to the constant omnipresent digital invitation. It is not solely symbolic but can help develop communion with God. These actions center our bodies. This means we root ourselves in our body itself and root it in the divine, too. When we enter these spaces I have spoken about and then begin to sit attentively, we realize that we are able to be present to the world and to the divine.

Resistance Recap: Digital Detox and Prayer

In an effort to combat the negative effects of technology overload, let's explore some digital detox practices. Findings from the University of Derby in 2016 and the American Psychological Association in 2017 show that limiting screen time and regularly stepping away from digital devices can benefit mental health. Scheduling digital detox into the daily routine by switching off one's phone at dining times, during prayer periods, or before sleep can greatly ease stress and enhance concentration.

As a Christian, I call this time for prayer, contemplation, and meditation. You can think of these as different fasting times for a deeper relationship with

God and others. Digital fasting can be a conscious break from devices over a given period to heighten awareness of and engagement with the material world and aid spiritual practices. Such fasting parallels the ancient Christian tradition of fasting from food to sustain an undivided attention toward God. Here are those practical recommendations.

Weekly Digital Sabbath: Devote one day each week—a "digital Sabbath"—to turn off all electronic devices and then spend time outdoors, be physically active, and participate in some spiritual discipline such as prayer, reading scripture, or worship. St. Anthony the Great, in the third century, and the later Desert Fathers removed themselves into the desert to live in isolated prayer and fasting to get away from the busyness to be closer to God. Believers today can do the same by logging off.

Take a breath now.

I know what I am saying may be distressing. I recognize the feeling of addiction to connectivity. That is what you are experiencing now. You are also running through the thousands of reasons you must be connected. However, the constant connectivity has created this reactivity. For over ten million years, people have lived successfully without telephones or smartphones. If you are an adult born prior to 1995, your parents did not know where you were at every moment of the day, and work stopped at 5:00 pm. There was no communication from work after work hours. Human beings can live without constant connectivity. However, we have unwillingly created an addiction that is the same as all addictions. Three suggestions for you: 1) have a close person be online for emergency calls; 2) let people know you are turning off your phone; and 3) take small steps and start with the next step first.

Daily Digital Fasts: Implement shorter digital fasts daily, such as turning off media devices during meals, in the morning before starting the day, or in the evening before bedtime.

Holy scriptures tell the story of Jesus's fasting in the wilderness (Matthew 4:1–11, Luke 4:1–13). Digital fasting can be modeled on Jesus's example by going into the wilderness (away from any city, especially one you live in), fasting, and meditating on God and wisdom texts. Jesus did so at the beginning of his ministry to reenergize his spiritual life. What we see of Jesus is that through his practice of prayer, he can withstand the promise of worldly seductions. Daily fasts create space to pray, think, and talk with others in ways that become more deliberate. Instead of mindlessly checking our phones, we can choose mindfully to meditate, rest, read, or pray silently. This is where being away from the desk or in front of the screen is helpful. Here are opportunities, even briefly, to find a space for silent attentiveness.

You can also include in this detox and fasting practice a buildup of regular daily prayer time in that space discussed earlier—your sacred space. I promise you that carving out a part of your day to be present will benefit you. Setting regular prayer times at the same time each day helps to create a rhythm of spiritual focus. Whether it is prayer at dawn, midday, or evening, the rhythm marks the time of day, setting a tempo for the day and providing a regular period to refocus our attention on

God. These periodic times can be creatively enriched by adding bodily elements, such as lighting a candle, kneeling during prayer, or using prayer beads.

Our current schedules are not working for us. The constant barrage of information, much of which is completely unnecessary, is part of the problem. How many of us pick up our phone as the first act of the day? What a difference if the first act were a quiet contemplation of gratitude. This does not have to be complicated. We make it all too complicated. Lay there, sit on the side of the bed, and begin by saying, "Thank you."

Spiritually, the distractions and the disembodiment of the digital pacify our spiritual imagination and, with it, our spiritual practices. Technologically, these are all just human-created tools. There is nothing inherently evil about them or creating them. It is the powers and principalities who use them to commoditize our bodies and affections while also our willingness to worship by giving time, money, and energy into the frame of the Internet and social media. It is us and our poor use of the tool that makes the tool anti-spiritual. The more we spend time interacting in digital space, the more we are deprived of the opportunities for embodied presence that helps us experience the fullness of spiritual life. The loss of both bodily presence and bodily interaction in a life lived in sacred spaces and prayer leads to the flattening of spiritual life. It becomes just another analog version of something we can be curious about. There is less and less attentiveness by our mind to our body and between our body and the divine.

It's important to remember the role of spiritual resistance, the active and deliberate reappropriation of our attention, and our embodied spiritual practices. Digital fasting, times for prayer, and daily rituals of mindful attention can help protect us against the consequences of digital life. Through these acts of resistance, we reorient ourselves toward our humanity and our shared life as human beings.

Chapter Three

God Dwelt Among Us: Embodiment

Resistance: Meditation

God became flesh and lived among us—
not in some abstract notion, but as an expression
of radical solidarity with human weakness.
Our breathing, posture and every step are
an opposition to disembodiment,
reverence all bodies as holy mirrors of God's revelation.
—A. D.

You may be reading this and are not an Episcopalian or even a Christian. Maybe you would define yourself as an agnostic, an atheist, a spiritual seeker, one of my siblings from the Abrahamic faiths, or someone who is looking to renew your faith in some way, and hoped this book was for you. Let me assure you that I am so happy you are reading this book, and I hope it will give you insight into resisting the anti-spiritual forces in your life. My sense of resistance is deeply woven into who I am in my tradition—in my unabashed faith. This has to do with my belief that God came in the person of Jesus, and that is where my theological roots in embodiment are bound.

In my faith tradition, we use the term *the Incarnation*—the belief that the Word of God became flesh in the person of Jesus, a central and profound mystery. So, let us hold that word *mystery* together for a bit. This mystery is the touch point between humans and the divine. The singularity of the human being Jesus is not merely a theological concept. It speaks to the heart of being human, touching on themes of embodiment, vulnerability, and divine presence.

Many ways to discuss this mystery include words such as *Word, Son,* and *Logos*. For now, let us use the *mystery of Jesus*. We believe that God became embodied. This mystery is so central that God's engagement with humans is good news. However, as a mystery, it does not work if God remains un-embodied. God chose to become present in bodily form and dwell within creation in a new and different way. Over so many years of our tradition, we have discovered that this mystery of Jesus continues to reveal who we are and how we share our bodies and experiences in creation with others.

Moreover, by living and praying with Jesus in mind, we resist actions that demean human dignity. Through the mystery of Jesus, we reject anti-human and anti-spiritual forces and have an opportunity to live more beloved human lives. We know, though, that we Christians are just like everyone else and find this very difficult indeed. Nevertheless, humankind, revealed in this way, shows that there is not one denomination, race, creed, language, or color, but rather that there is solidarity among all humanity due to this mystery of Jesus.

Theologian Rowan Williams offers in his work that through the centrality of this mystery, we may experience a profound change in our perspective because of an act of a God who shared humanity with us. We, in turn, discover that despite all our failure to love and care for each other and to seek the divine with our whole body, we can still find each other in the mystery of Jesus. Despite all the categories we make up, we have an opportunity to see in each other a creative inspiration to bless each other and bless God in a life of offering.

The purpose of embodiment through individual and corporate life, sometimes called church, is to dwell in and create sacred space as a form of resistance. In that space, we are to model bodily mutuality, human dignity, and hospitality and see that difference is nothing more than a human skill of categorization.

At the same time, various kinds of embodiment are beautiful fingerprints of the divine. Jesus's life of offering was such that if we attempted a similar thing, we may find ourselves in uncomfortable new spaces. Through the disciplines of resistance we can see the center of God surrounding us in the comfort of a lovely embrace. We discover through meditation and contemplative prayer that to live an embodied life of love creates new faithful communities. Let's explore embodiment more and the practices that come with it before we get to the aspect of communal life.

The bodies we see with finite limitations and fragile vulnerability are all included in the mystery of Jesus's body. This is inclusive of but not limited to the Christian understanding of the cross of Jesus. This idea is more than the physical fleshiness of our actual bodies; it includes the mystery of our human nature marked by its vulnerability and finitude.

When we unpack the idea of God's presence in the mystery of Jesus, we might think of words, prayers, and passages from the Bible that speak about God dwelling among us. The dwelling of the mystery of Jesus is like our faith ancestors' experience of God, who pitched in the tent among the people to be present in their midst. In my tradition, God is not a remote, abstract God, but immediately present and touching the circumstances of our everyday human being and bodily experiences.

Another notion of the mystery of Jesus's dwelling embodied with us is God's eternity. Perhaps you have heard the term *thin spaces* before. Thin spaces are what we are working to create in this practice of resistance. We are endeavoring in public Christian worship, as in this practice of contemplation and meditation, to participate in the thin space of eternity. In this context, our tradition speaks about Jesus's eternal embodiment using the title *Christ,* which refers to the mystery of Jesus's body and eternal being.

An Expanded Embodiment

This exploration seeks to imagine a more nuanced and capacious theology that unsettles traditional theological categories. In so doing we engage ways of imagining what it means for all human bodies to be made in the image of the mystery of Christ's eternal embodiment, from which the cosmos was modeled and to which the cosmos returns.

Lisa Powell, in her work *The Disabled God* and some of her other writings, extends the discussion on the theology of the body by exploring the implications of the mystery of Jesus for understanding human dignity, particularly in the context of disability. This feels important in this chapter because before we move to an introduction of the practice of the presence of God, we need to acknowledge that the embodiment of Jesus compels us to consider Powell's thinking. Powell challenges traditional theological perspectives that prioritize spiritual perfection over physical embodiment. She argues that the mystery of Jesus's resurrection affirms the value of all bodies, including those that are disabled, wounded, or otherwise considered "imperfect" by societal standards (Powell, 2024).

Given how I have described the mystery of Jesus, her critique of spiritualized interpretations of the resurrection insists, as I have, that resurrection promises the redemption of the entire person, the entire body and soul—affirming the dignity of embodied life. Her work challenges us to rethink our attitudes toward all bodies, especially in a culture that often devalues physical weakness or difference.

Consider the work of John Hull, who has written on blind theology over and against a kind of accepted ocular-centrism. He does this in his two books, *Notes on Blindness* and *In the Beginning There Was Darkness* (Hull, 2017, 2002). Part of what he and other authors on this subject do is show that all bodies matter to our theological conversation in a positive and contributory way. We must question the supremacy of vision in our understandings of faith, spirituality, and religious encounters with God while confronting the unexamined assumption that sight is the preeminent sense through which we are to approach and engage our encounters with the world and God. Visionary theology, using visual imagery, symbols, and metaphors that appeal to the sense of sight, retains its place within the church's liturgical practices.

Blind theology advocates for more opportunities to enrich liturgy with other sensory experiences that are less reliant on the eye, as well as encouraging the church to appreciate the spiritual insights that a blind person can bring into the theological arena.

In a way, deaf theology also breathes new life and a new dimension into our concepts of communication, prayer, meditation, and revelation. Here, I am influenced by the work of Wayne Morris, who wrote *Theology without Words* (Morris, 2016). Working with a tradition emphasizing the centrality of "the Word," deaf theology encourages us to think about how God's Word is communicated and received non-verbally. It asks us to explore how God's Word can be channeled through sign language and visual modes of communication. It presses us toward a new way of thinking about prayer's embodied dimension and how various forms of prayer and worship reflect the plurality of God's creation.

After reading Phoebe Caldwell's book *Finding You, Finding Me* (2006) and living life with neurodivergent parishioners across my diocese, I have come to realize I must be attentive so they may bless me by opening up my mind to new ways of imagining theology and prayer. Neurodivergent people, expressly but not limited to those with autism, ADHD, and dyslexia, create an opportunity to reflect on the requirement of stillness for contemplation and meditation. Indeed, I have known this was true since I learned how to pray. We must understand that prayer and contemplation may cast off the restrictive movement-inhibiting wrappings and that we might learn from our brothers, sisters, and siblings that by giving way, we discover something more fluid and reparative. Neurodivergence reminds us that there is no "normal" or "standard" way of thinking, perceiving, or interacting with the world (Maté & Maté, 2022). Cognitive difference is a gift that invites us to ponder new possibilities as novices in the work of prayer that is also resistance against anti-spiritual and anti-bodily influences.

In this way, our theology of prayer is enlarged by an understanding of God's diverse creation. God does not believe anyone is "less than" or "not crucial" to our life together because of difference. In this context, we may cultivate a greater understanding of the sensitivities of sensory overload or other experiences that neurodivergent bodies might face, as well as being open to the gifting of who they are within the sacred community of life lived together.

These views also serve to remind us that the diversity of the human body is not accidental but reflects instead the greater harmony where difference is understood as a human societal tool, and where love is God's spiritually unifying act of embodiment. The mystery of Jesus and what we call the Incarnation is thus recovered in a cumulative way to account for God's cognizance of the embodied human beings, such that bodies, irrespective of physical or sensory ability or cognitive difference, are nonetheless each "fearfully and wonderfully made" (Psalm 139:14). Such a conclusion has consequences for the recovery of the language of the resurrected body (Powell, 2024), as I have shown; perhaps more important, we may learn that it has the power to help us think more broadly about our practice of the presence of God.

Resistance Recap: Sitting in Contemplation and Meditation: A Guide

Contemplation or meditation can be viewed as both an art and a discipline. I can only share what I have been given. I can only offer you what I have failed and learned. I can only share with you the deep wisdom of my teachers. The bibliography contains a list of books that you might refer to and are written by wise and learned practitioners of this most ancient art.

With that, I turn to how to sit, attend to your body, quiet your mind's chatter, and lead yourself step by step toward an experience of more profound connectedness. The benefits of learning these basic steps can be immense and far-reaching in your life. There are ways to prepare your body for contemplation and meditation, drawing on exercises from the Christian mystical tradition (including the theologian Thomas Merton and the book *The Cloud of Unknowing*). I will also share how my contemplative practice has improved through conversation and practice with Buddhist friends who encourage mindful sitting and walking.

The Art of Sitting: Turn Your Phone Off

This step is obvious. Turn the haptics off, and power down if you can. I am in churches all the time, and you would think that after twenty years, we would know how to do this, but alas, we forget. If God is going to speak to you, God does not need a device. Turning your phone off is step one.

The Art of Sitting: Find Your Posture

I once had a professor who told me a story about how hard he practiced before his first meeting with a virtuoso cello instructor and what he learned after playing his heart out. The instructor said kindly and wisely when he was finished, "Let us begin with how you are seated." So, we begin with posture. Your physical posture in meditation matters greatly.

Let us first consider *posture* as a general term for how you sit. It is how the Orthodox seminarian so many years ago taught me how to sit when I was a restless twenty-something. We seek a body posture that is wakeful and clear but not stressed. Thomas Merton argued this point when he wrote that preserving wakefulness is all about sitting upright, which allows the contemplative to feel rooted and open to their experience (Merton, 1986). *Seeds of Contemplation* was one of the first books my friend told me to read. The second was *The Cloud of Unknowing,* written by an unknown author sometime in the fourteenth century. I have a worn-out Penguin classic version (Anon, 1961). Zen master Thich Nhất Hạnh said that Buddhists across the spectrum will attest that a settled body promotes a quiet mind and an open heart alike (Nhất Hạnh, 1991).

For those of you who wish to sit, go to that place where you will sit, that sacred space you created in your home, garden, park, synagogue, mosque, or church. Some of you will want to sit on a cushion, in a chair, or upon the ground directly. Go there as close as you can to your appointed time. There will be interruptions, but you will learn in time to move in mediation through them and not be sent careening off into wakefulness. Sit comfortably, with your back in a position of wakefulness and not sleepiness; let your shoulders drop, and relax your hands by allowing the weight to drop onto your lap. Let your neck relax and your face fall to a comfortable position.

Next, close your eyes. This can be very helpful for those new to the practice. Closing one's eyes is not required. Contemplation upon images or scenery can be part of your style of prayer. You may always find closing your eyes is good. Routine is best; nothing is necessary. Necessity and perfection are the enemies of contemplation. We are attempting to learn how to pray and become attentive.

The Art of Sitting: Breathing with Awareness

Everyone breathes differently. Breathing is a part of our body's every-minute function, and it is so automatic that you must think about it to notice it. Breathing is integral to your body's particular prayer and attentiveness. After comfortably finding your posture and closing your eyes, the next thing you will do is notice your breathing. This is more than paying attention to it with your mind. I want you to feel your body and how so many parts move slightly when you breathe.

If you have come rushing to do your meditation and find that you are breathless or breathing heavily, start again with sitting. Move from adjusting your comfortable posture to paying more and more attention to your breathing. As your body, shoulders, hands, legs, and internal organs find their equilibrium in your posture, your breathing will naturally slow down.

Breathe deeply several times, slowly inhaling through your nose and exhaling through your mouth, and let your breath find its pace. As you breathe, become aware of what you feel in your body—the rising and falling of your chest, the cool air moving into your nostrils and the warmed breath as you exhale through your mouth. Appreciate how it feels to have an experience of breath.

The Art of Sitting: Feeling the Body

As time passes, you may find yourself drifting into your body. When this happens, you can go deeper into feeling your body. This is sometimes called a "body scan" in many traditions.

A body scan begins by paying attention to the top of your head, working your way down through your body, noticing where you feel tightness or discomfort. You can scan the physical areas of your forehead, eyes, jaw, neck, shoulders, arms, torso, legs, and feet, breathing into them and allowing them to relax. This helps ground you in the present moment and prepares your body for even more profound meditation. Merton often spoke about the value of bodily awareness in a contemplative context as something that helps you relate to God in God's fullness. To feel your body is a resistant act to the disembodied screen and constant connectivity of our lives.

Sit for a while in this bodily attentiveness to posture, breath, and sensation. Let this state last as long as you can. When distracted, come back to it. First, begin with five minutes of sitting as a goal, but take what you can get. If you go longer, that is good too. My goal is to sit for twenty minutes a day. I also sit for moments throughout the day—I grab these out of my busy schedule. I end the night with a quiet prayer. I can sit for an hour or longer after years of practice and enjoy doing so when I am in a sacred space, most especially where the walls are bathed with the prayers of people. You are yoking yourself to a daily life of prayer (this is the meaning of the word *yoga*—to be yoked in a practice of meditation).

The Art of Walking Meditation

For those with difficulty sitting, walking meditation allows the cultivation of a contemplative practice without needing a chair or a cushion. In the Christian tradition of labyrinths, we use walking meditation to practice the presence of God. It is often walked on a maze on the floor, as in many cathedrals worldwide. In the Middle Ages, it was a safe way to make a pilgrimage to God and the Holy Land without traveling too far from home.

To find a labyrinth in proximity to where you live, use this website: https://labyrinthlocator.org/. However, walking meditation is available to you wherever you are.

After years of practicing meditation, I took several classes on walking and sitting from a Buddhist. I was having a hard time walking the labyrinth and keeping my attentiveness. So, I hoped I would learn how to walk and pray at the same time. Just as breathing is movement, and the body moves when you breathe, the whole body's movement is merely an expansion of movement and prayer.

You can do this in your sacred space, as we discussed, but you may want more room. So, outside gardens and sacred spaces may be better for this practice, though if you have a big room, that will work, too. I have practiced this in art galleries worldwide, so this type of meditation travels well.

Stand still, then walk, lifting your feet one at a time and feel the earth beneath them. When you begin to walk, do so in time with your breathing—lift one foot as you inhale, and set it down intentionally, then your other foot as you exhale. Become aware of your feet lifting, your legs moving, and your breathing in and out. Practice this until your mind quiets. The key here is the feeling of the sole of your shoe lifting from contact with the earth. I found this an essential piece of coaching as a novice walker because I would often find my attentiveness wane, and I would begin to pick up speed. I have found you can always return to your sole and the earth, your soul and God's creation.

The mystery of Jesus, the Incarnation, is a central theological pillar that undergirds the resistance to disembodiment. It speaks to my tradition's understanding of God, the human body, and its essential humanness. This is essential when we speak of the eternal nature of the mystery of Jesus for this reason. For in the eternal nature of this mystery, we discover every human body; because God has taken on a body, it means that resistance is not merely for this world but brings the fullness of our relationship with the eternal divine into our present bodily state.

The Incarnation lies at the center of all Christian theology. It is the belief that God embraces the human body and human nature so closely and tightly that God wrapped himself in flesh and blood in Jesus of Nazareth.

This act of divine embodiment has reoriented the definition of what it means to be a human body. So, we are reminded to inhabit spaces by valuing all bodies.

Chapter Four

All Bodies Are Prophets of Resistance

Resistance: Prayer

We should ask ourselves: What part of our embodied humanity have we sacrificed to the human-designed leviathan of technology? Prophets invite us to turn away from the ever-present screen to the quiet freedom where body and mind can breathe.
—A. D.

Today, in the age of information technology, the Internet of Things (IoT) dominates both the conscious mind and human beings' day-to-day lives. The effects of its daily interaction and influence on the body, which includes the mind and nervous system, are sometimes exceedingly integrated. This is what some are calling supra-consciousness. There is much conversation about the ubiquity of technology. Consider the annual growth and percentage of all human bodies connected to screens and technology.

At the beginning of July 2024, 5.45 billion people worldwide were using the Internet, which is 67.1 percent of the world's population. This eye-popping figure translates to the fact that, at present, internet users are a supermajority: there are now more than twice as many people using the Internet as not. The number of people on the Internet is also rising. Figures for July 2024 show that the world-connected population increased by 167 million users in the previous twelve months. While not as high as the peak growth of the last decade, 3.2 percent, the preceding numbers remain a high growth rate (Kemp, 2024). What is interesting about this number is that given the growth and decline expected by 2100, it will most likely reach over 85 percent of the world's population. There are many factors affecting this future number: technological, economic, and social barriers (population data for this rate projection was from Pew Research; see Cilluffo, 2019).

Once we consider the number of people who are today and will in the future be connected, it is essential to ask what the impact upon the body is, beyond the act of working, searching, and creating via technology.

This chapter will explore the neurological and chemical effects of electronic device usage with the aim of understanding how bodies (including the brain and nervous system) are fundamentally shaped by the constant interaction with and manipulation of electronic devices. Furthermore, we continue to unearth the active transmutative form of prayer and meditation for body and soul. We look at the multiple short-term and long-term benefits of meditation and prayer and their profound and subtle effects on the body—the person as a whole.

In many religious traditions, including my own, we share the story of Elijah on Mount Carmel from the first book of Kings, chapter eighteen. It is about a prophet who is victorious against other prophets. I am playing here with the idea of the promises of technology and artificial intelligence versus the promises of prayer and contemplation—the forms resistant to anti-spiritual influences.

The Neurological and Chemical Impacts of Electronic Device Usage

In the 1990s, Kalle Lasn wrote several books, including *Culture Jam* (1999) and *Meme Wars* (2013). In *Culture Jam,* he wrote a little paragraph, which I have used several times over the last twenty-six years. I noticed that people back in the 1990s didn't understand Lasn, and today the same paragraph resonates with so many people as if he were a prophet himself. In 1999, he described exactly what many parents describe to me when their kids have devices removed from their environment. They cannot seem to survive without them (Lasn, 1999, 3-4).

What happens to our bodies when we connect through various forms of technology? The pervasive use of electronic devices significantly impacts our neurological processes and bodily chemistry. The prefrontal cortex, responsible for decision-making, attention, and complex cognitive behaviors, is heavily engaged during electronic device tasks. This constant engagement can lead to "cognitive overload," where the brain becomes over-stimulated, reducing efficiency and increasing errors (Prensky, 2001). Simultaneously, dopaminergic pathways (neurons that travel through the brain and produce dopamine) are activated, particularly when engaging with rewarding content such as social media. This leads to the release of dopamine, a neurotransmitter associated with motivation and pleasure, which reinforces the behavior and can contribute to addictive patterns (Berridge & Robinson, 2016).

The amygdala, involved in emotional processing, becomes more active when interacting with emotionally charged content online. This heightened activation can lead to stronger emotional responses and increased stress levels (LaBar & Phelps, 1998).

Many findings like the cortisol levels and heart rate data are currently being studied—with different outcomes; however, high melatonin levels due to screen time remain supported by research. The research suggests that extended screen time, especially at night, can disrupt serotonin production by affecting melatonin levels, leading to sleep disturbances and mood regulation issues (Blume et al., 2019; Nagare et al., 2019).

These findings illustrate the profound effects of electronic device usage on mental and physical health, emphasizing the need for mindful engagement with technology to mitigate potential negative consequences. The wisdom of meditation and prayer is so important to your body because it affects the nervous system in so many observable and beneficial ways.

We cannot simply speak of the connection between the mind and technology, because that is too narrow. Similarly, it affects more than our consciousness. Our bodies are profoundly connected, but not in a Newtonian or even neo-Newtonian manner of physical forces reacting to each other. Our bodies are impacted by the invisible forces between the body and mechanical and human tools created to make life enjoyable, create new work, and simplify the lives of human beings. What is happening is much more than what meets human observation. We cannot fathom the interactive nature of our body and its complex internal synergistic systems.

Long-Term Physical and Mental Effects of Electronic Device Usage

Not only are things connected and interactive in the moment, but we can also understand the long-term effects of these interactions. While technology offers numerous benefits, the constant connectivity and prolonged screen time associated with electronic device usage can lead to significant health issues.

One of the most concerning long-term effects is cognitive decline and memory impairment. Prolonged multitasking and reliance on digital tools can impair the brain's ability to focus intensely and retain information. This leads to attention deficits and a phenomenon known as "digital amnesia," where memory processes weaken due to the easy accessibility of information online (Robert & Kadhiravan, 2022).

Another critical area affected is mental health. Increased risk of anxiety and depression are common consequences of chronic electronic device usage. The overstimulation of the brain's reward system, mainly through social media, can create a cycle of craving and withdrawal, contributing to mood disorders. Additionally, the constant release of cortisol due to stress from digital engagement can damage the brain's emotional regulation centers in the long term (Vorster-De Wet, et al., 2023). Other published research shows that the decrease of these effects occurs when electronic device use is decreased (Pedersen et al., 2022).

Sleep disorders also appear to have ravaged heavy electronic device users. Prolonged screen time, especially before going to bed, results in a disruption of circadian rhythms, causing insomnia and poor sleep quality. This, in turn, can lead to a host of health problems, including impaired immune function and a greater risk of cardiovascular diseases. To be clear, the mechanism linking to these last-named effects is an indirect one via other health drivers (Devi & Singh, 2023).

Physical health is also adversely affected. Digital eye strain, slouching over handheld devices, and the flow-on effects of continued sedentariness from prolonged screen exposure have been linked to lifestyle-related chronic conditions, such as musculoskeletal problems, type 2 diabetes, and cardiovascular disease (Devi & Singh, 2023).

It's an issue that affects social health too. Not only does excessive screen time, particularly among younger users, lead to a lifetime of social isolation, it can also damage social skills. Lacking enough face-to-face interaction and relying on digital communication can strain personal relationships and impede the development of social skills (Zubair et al., 2023).

Long-term use of electronic devices can cause neurochemical imbalances. Stimulating brain reward pathways continuously can lead to dopamine desensitization, which decreases the brain's ability to feel pleasure naturally and increases the risk of addictive behaviors. Chronic stress and poor sleep can also spur chronic inflammation and worsen new health risks.

Constant and some might say obsessive contact on social media could invariably lead, as the years go by, to these individuals' suffering from emotional and mental health issues denting their quality of life. These long-term effects stress the importance of regulating how we use technology and the importance of striking a balance between screen time and activities that foster good physical and mental health. As the implications become more apparent, we cannot ignore these issues if we are to curb the impact of technology and uphold mental and physical health in the digital age (Speranza et al., 2021; Chen et al., 2023).

The Choice of Prophet Is Yours

I suggest that you choose which prophet you will listen to and be as your life unfolds before you. Let me tell you an old story dating back thousands of years related to a prophet, Elijah, whom I mentioned earlier. If you are a Bible reader, you can read the text in 1 Kings 18. Elijah is deeply connected to God; he listens, prays, and speaks to the people out of this deep connection. There is a problem in their society. The people adopted a new way of living that included allegiance to a lesser god, believing that this god would bring about good things for all the people. Things were not good, though, so the rulers and people worshiped the lesser god even more. There was a drought, and the lesser god's prophets promised that the earth god they were worshiping would bring rain.

You can see that the story explains people's unfaithfulness. I believe what happens in humans is this: We get all tied up with the idea of earthly power and wealth, and we start sacrificing to lower-case gods of all kinds, like money, work, entertainment, "likes," sports, and success. It rarely works out.

So Elijah, I paraphrase, says, "Okay, you all, let's do this right. Nothing is working for you, but you have forgotten that God has already provided the way of doing things that will truly benefit the whole people." Elijah doubles down on an examination of prophetic power. He says, "Let's battle this out. Let's have an open contest on the mountain of Carmel. If your god is so good for you, we will see if it is provable (paraphrase)."

Next, the prophets of the lower-case god, and the people, show up in mass—450 strong. It is as if the prophets are saying to Elijah, "Look, this stuff is so good, see how many people believe in the deliverance of our god." Meanwhile, Elijah is by his lonesome. Right out of a Western movie, Elijah stands on the hill as a stark expression of the enormous odds stacked against him. Of course, after they go first, nothing happens. They may do all kinds of acts and cast all sorts of spells. Nothing happens. There is no rain. Elijah taunts them, "Call louder! Cry out! Perhaps your little god of promises is lost in thought, or he is on a journey. But wake him up (paraphrase)!" Nothing happens again and again.

What Elijah, the prophet, does is make an altar to God in the middle of the people, creating sacred space. At that moment, Elijah has an exacting calm and opens himself to the divine by redirecting his and the people's hearts to the true God. Of course, God acts and responds by showing the power of this relationship. So, the people understand the prophetic witness of Elijah and the essential connection to the divine.

People will take this part of God's narrative in many ways. As someone who cares for people, I find it speaks deeply to how humans fall for easy and earthly promises.

It is part of our longing for something beyond ourselves. It is about that missing bit of us only completed by God.

I care about how technology is affecting our human bodies. There is no question that the IoT epoch is promising new wealth, new economies of scale, and creative technologies that can solve many problems. Like all the other lower-case gods before it, it will profit the wealthy proportionately more than the average person. Yet, it comes with a cost. All consumption of things by our bodies comes with a price that will be paid eventually. We are consuming this technology without attentiveness. The prophets of the promise of technology have made their case. The researchers as prophets have repeatedly shown the toll their tech takes on our human body.

I have already written about creating a sacred space in the mountain of our lives. I have talked about setting aside holy time. I have also explored some ways we can resist these prophets of false gods: excessive consumerism, round-the-clock work schedules, misdirected ideas of success. What we are talking about is the long-term benefit of resistance, of creating sacred space, settling into sacred time, and working on sacred practices. This is the resistance of a well-lived prayer life that transforms and even heals the body.

The Immediate Effects of Prayer and Meditation on the Mind and Body

Prayer and meditation have been practiced for centuries across various cultures and religions, especially among the Abrahamic faiths. Many people know of Buddhist contemplation and meditation techniques; however, Christianity, Judaism, and Islam each have ancient practices of meditation. Modern research increasingly supports the positive impact of prayer on both the mind and body. This section explores the immediate effects of these practices, focusing on how they influence brain function, physiological responses, and overall well-being.

Brain Activation and Neurochemical Changes

A study by Andrew Newberg and colleagues discovered increased activity in the prefrontal cortex (the same part of the brain that technology lights up) of people who meditated, but with different results (Newberg, 2014). Prayer and meditation stimulate the frontal lobe, especially the prefrontal cortex, the elaborate crest of high-order neurons at the brain's peak that is linked to attention, focus, and executive function. This leads to better concentration and increases overall self-awareness.

Increased Alpha and Theta Brain Waves

A study in the journal *Cognitive Brain Research* found that long-term meditators had increased alpha and theta wave activity during meditation, indicating greater inner calm. We learn that meditation, particularly mindfulness and deep breathing exercises, increases alpha and theta brain wave activity. Alpha waves indicate relaxed wakefulness; theta waves, deep relaxation and creativity (Raymond et al., 2005).

Dopamine and Serotonin Release, and Decrease in Cortisol Levels

The release of neurotransmitters, such as dopamine and serotonin, linked to feelings of well-being and euphoria, has been reported to occur during prayer and meditation. This explains the immediate sense of calm or emotional stability often reported accompanying these practices. The research also shows that more than just the well-being of the body is at stake, as prayer contributes to immune functions within the body (Davidson et al., 2003). By alleviating stress and the cycle of inflammation, one can reduce one's risk of heart disease. Several studies show yoga decreases blood pressure (Cramer et al., 2014; Mizuno & Monteiro, 2013). In addition, when people pray or meditate, their cortisol levels are lower, reducing stress and anxiety (Mizuno & Monteiro, 2013).

Enhanced Immune Function

With specific intent, a simple meditation or prayer can affect the immune system almost immediately: stress hormones are soothed, calm is restored, and the system can function well with the defenses it has. The body keeps a natural baseline state of good health and can deal with minor infections and colds. Studies show that prayer and meditation prolong life in many ways (Andrade & Radhakrishnan, 2009). One study showed that people with HIV lived seventeen years longer than their peers when they prayed and meditated. This included when their friends prayed for them too (Ironson & Ahmad, 2022). Studies and journals show through peer-reviewed research that while prolonged use of technology will increase immediate and long-term bodily problems, prayer and meditation are an antidote and have a well-being effect on the human body.

Beyond this, prayer and meditation are associated with the following positive effects on the body and relationships: improved mood, enhanced cognitive function, improved attention, mental clarity, reduction in mind wandering, decline in anxiety, a decline in fear, more balanced emotions, sense of personal purpose, and feelings of security. Moreover, many studies have found that prayer and meditation have long-term effects like longer life, better cognition, and slowed cognitive decline (Lazar et al., 2005).

Loving Kindness and Loneliness

In a world filled with fear, loneliness, and need, along with a global concern for our future, prayer increases feelings of compassion, connection, kindness, and care for others. We might call this the practice of loving-kindness in prayer. Meditation opens our hearts to love others. I admire this saying from the Society of St. John's founder Richard Meaux Benson, who said, "When you take a person's name with you into your prayer to God who is love, how can you not come to learn to love that person." Meditation makes you feel more connected to others, better able to be warm and friendly and see the dignity in others.

A 2008 study by Barbara Fredrickson at the University of North Carolina reported that participants who practiced loving-kindness meditation reported more positive emotions three weeks later, along with warmth, care, and connection toward others (Fredrickson et al., 2008). Similar studies show increases in care for oneself and others in people with posttraumatic stress, especially veterans, and that this further predicted future well-being outcomes.

Prayer and meditation also increase the sense of serving, helping, and caring for others. Research shows how prayer changes us to care for those beyond tribal groups (Zheng et al., 2023). This connects to the notion that through prayer we improve our connection with the divine, heal our bodies, and begin to heal society.

These long-term rewards attest to the far-reaching ripple effects of regular prayer and meditation on the body and mind. In the future, as we deepen our understanding of these practices as techniques of spiritual resistance and life-building tools, we will see more clearly that prayer and meditation resist distraction and constant connectivity while creating sustained health, wholeness, and spiritual depth.

Resistance Recap: Entering Contemplation: The Quiet Mind

In the quiet moments of contemplation and the stillness of meditation, we encounter a profound truth: All bodies, regardless of ability or difference, can resist the forces that seek to marginalize and exclude. This chapter explores how various forms of meditation and spiritual practice can be adapted to include everyone, from those who are deaf or blind to individuals with neurodivergent conditions or physical disabilities. By embracing the diverse ways bodies move, sense, and experience the world, we can create inclusive spaces where spiritual resistance is not just possible but also profoundly transformative.

Throughout history, many traditions, including Christianity, have valued silence and stillness as powerful tools for connecting with the divine. These practices are not reserved for a select few but are accessible to all, provided we are willing to adapt and honor the unique needs of different bodies. Whether through visual focus for the deaf, tactile elements for blind people, or dynamic practices for the neurodivergent, each person can find a way to engage deeply with their spiritual life.

What follows is a guide through practical ways to create inclusive meditation spaces, offering insights into how intention, community, and the physical environment can support a more embodied approach to spirituality. By doing so, we affirm that everybody can participate in resistance to the isolation, marginalization, and disembodiment that the present technological age often imposes. These practices give us the power to reclaim our humanness and strengthen our communal bonds.

As we delve into the contemplative practices that foster this resistance, we are reminded that silence, stillness, and focused intention are not the absence of action. Prayer is the foundation of a life lived in conscious opposition to the forces that diminish our humanity. Together, let us explore how all bodies can participate in this sacred act of resistance, finding strength in our diversity and unity in our shared spiritual journey.

Embracing Silence

The Christian tradition has practiced the quality of silence as a prized means to an end in the metaphysical context of finding all the goodness I have spoken about, including the connection with the divine. From *The Cloud of Unknowing*:

> If you wish to enter into this cloud, to be at home in it, and to take up the contemplative work of love as I urge you to, there is something else you must do. Just as the cloud of unknowing lies above you, between you and your God, you must fashion a cloud of forgetting beneath you, between you and every created thing. The cloud of unknowing will perhaps leave you with the feeling that you are far from God. But no, if it is authentic, only the absence of a cloud of forgetting keeps you from him now. . . . To put it briefly, during this work, you must abandon them all beneath the cloud of forgetting (Anonymous, Chapter 5, 1961).

If you're sitting, sit there. If you are walking, walk. As thoughts come up, allow them to come and go without attaching to or judging them, without chastising yourself for having an idea, without picking up any thoughts and running with them. Just allow these thoughts to come and go, always returning to the breath. The object is not to force the mind into silence. It is to allow the mind to come to a silent state. You are coming into the awareness of God's presence as your mind quiets.

The Role of Intention

I have found over and over again that intention is as essential as attention. Practice with the intent of communion with the divine, with God, that which is the singularity beyond all of the cosmos and also embraces all the cosmos. Thomas Merton spoke of this in spiritual terms, referring to intellect, mind, and spirit (Merton, 1986). I suggest that the Christian intention is to seek the fullness of our bodies in order to come to our prayer time to connect to the God of day, night, and love. Here, we are creating, beyond the curation of space and time, a sacred reality with a character of betweenness. We are entering the in-betweenness of the body and the God of eternity.

Approaching Contemplation and Meditation with Different Bodies

Everybody is capable of resisting the power of anti-spiritual influences. For those who desire to be still and at peace, contemplation and meditation are personal explorations and practices that can be tailored to the unique needs of all bodies. Considerations and unique approaches can help make the practices accessible for those who are deaf, blind, in bodily pain, neurodivergent, or experiencing any bodily impairment.

Here are some ways to think about other possibilities for various bodies, beginning with deaf bodies. Meditation sessions that rely on auditory cues or speech are less accessible for individuals who are deaf or hard of hearing. Other senses, like the visual, can be emphasized to heighten the meditation experience—such as by focusing on visual elements. Candles, icons, handheld labyrinths, painted labyrinths, or any other still forms of beauty, such as flowers, clouds, or stones, can all be used as objects to facilitate meditation.

Despite a few periods in the Christian chronicle, our tradition has a long history of using aesthetic visual images for storytelling, prayer, and contemplation. There are many ways of undertaking a contemplative act of prayer using imagery. On an icon, as an example, the nose is an excellent place on which to focus.

A straightforward practice could involve sitting quietly and gazing at a lit candle or a sacred image. Focus on what is before you, contemplating the detail in the flicker of a flame or the hue and shape of a holy icon, and allow your mind to calm and your breath to regulate itself. Hold the image in your focus, deepening your breath and settling your mind. This simple and beautiful practice can be heightened when we choose personal symbols or objects that guide our reverent, emotional state as we meditate.

For people who are deaf or hard of hearing who use sign language, meditation can be a particularly appropriate time to mix the two by bringing the practice of signing into meditation. Just as one might contemplate an icon, one might consider holding in mind a phrase, word, or image of a word, or using one's hands to sign slowly and repetitively as a manner of embracing meditation.

Even writing the phrase or word can be an active form of contemplation. Intentional motion can be followed by emptiness; sound dissipates, and one begins to hear the echo, the reverb, deep in one's chest. The strokes of the hand guide the rhythm of the breath, and the wrist articulates the cadence. One holds the phrase in one's mind—treasuring it, savoring it—and repeats the mantra effortlessly, silently, and delightedly. It does not matter what the sound vocalized is. This goes against our idea of silence, but remember, we are finding ways all bodies can do this prayer of resistance.

I find it intriguing that silence has a special meaning for deaf people, just as movement has a different meaning for hearing people. For the hearing person, silence must be learned. For many deaf people, it is an ancient and natural ground.

The absence of external sounds increases the listener's awareness of what is happening internally. The deaf person can make of this silence not so much a noiseless state as a stillness, a sacred space open to God in which there is no noise to distract from hearing with one's heart. Practicing silence in the manner of the Gospel might be to sit in a comfortable chair, look toward the floor or ground, and then close the eyes and do nothing. As thoughts can be the loudest and most seductive noise for all bodies, one can briefly acknowledge their appearance, recognize them, and then let them go.

Incorporating tactile and kinesthetic elements is another prayer tool that all bodies can use. My father and I went on a ten-day walking pilgrimage when I was eleven. We received Catholic rosaries (as opposed to an Anglican rosary or Orthodox prayer beads) on that pilgrimage. They were blessed by Pope John Paul II. I memorized the prayers and, to this day, sometimes pray the Catholic rosary. Prayer beads are a tactile and kinesthetic prayer tool. Later, I learned how to pray with Orthodox prayer ropes of different types. In the mid 1980s, the Anglican rosary was created. For me, the Anglican rosary is too short; the Catholic rosary has a bit longer practice of prayer associated with it. I enjoy using the Orthodox prayer beads most. I find that sometimes tactile prayer helps many people to pray, while I acknowledge it may distract others.

For blind people, we might emphasize other senses to help with meditation. For people who do not see or do not see well, meditation can be vibrant and immersive for all the nonvisual senses. Those who are blind may prefer to do away with images altogether and focus instead on feeling, hearing, smelling, and the internal sense of bodily awareness.

Beyond the rosary, one can use texture to augment touch as a meditation focus. A stone or pebble the practitioner repeatedly holds and feels during meditation can stimulate calmer senses. A tactile concentration point can keep the seeker grounded in the present moment. The rubbing and manipulation of a tactile object can help focus the practitioner on meditating on these physical sensations and, by extension, the object's "presence" or symbolism. For instance, praying through a rosary might also create a rhythmic structure, with the tactile experience of each bead marking one breath, prayer, or moment of contemplation. Another example might be the handheld labyrinth. With a handheld labyrinth one may trace one's fingers through the design slowly and quietly.

Sound can be as central to meditation for the blind as sight might be for the sighted. A running stream, leaves rustling, or the ringing of a bell can provide an auditory focal point for meditation. Listening to psalms, hymns, sacred music, or drumming can deepen the experience and ease one into a meditative state. I have used the recorded prayer sounds from the Society of St. John the Evangelist in Boston, Massachusetts.

Those who pray often do not think about how vital smell can be. Our sense of smell reminds us of the fact we are talking about the whole body's being in prayer. The smell of incense can be used to anoint the act of meditation, as can essential oils or scented candles. Certain smells evoke specific spiritual feelings: frankincense for sacredness, lavender for calm, and citrus for invigoration. If noticed—really noticed—the scent can deepen awareness. By focusing on the smell, the sensory sphere becomes a means to steady the mind and open the heart to the presence of God. The smell can be particularly individualistic, and when we come to communal prayer, we need to remember that some people are sensitive to fragrance, which can make them ill.

Bodily awareness is a significant aspect of meditation. One can focus on the sensation of the air moving in and out of the body, the stimulus of the pulse beating within the chest, and the feeling of being held by the ground beneath one's feet. In this form of meditation, one becomes ever more aware of the body as a temple of the Holy Spirit.

Incorporating Braille and tactile texts is as essential for blind people as sign language can be for deaf people. For the Braille literate, tactile texts can provide an excellent form of meditation and prayer. Reading a portion of scripture, a prayer, or spiritual reflection in Braille can provide a focus for meditation and the opportunity to access a sacred text significantly. It can also allow the reader to experience the reading process slowly and meditatively, thus giving the Braille reader's body another opportunity to experience the material nature of Braille. This example illustrates how a tactile engagement with scripture or prayer can expand the practice of contemplation, making for a meditative session that remains contemplative and embodied. Similarly, a handheld labyrinth might be a way of tracing contemplatively.

Blind people can find the environment a guide to meditative fulfillment with soundscapes—the murmur of leaves in trees, the chatter of waves on a shore, the cries of birds—creating profound experiences of communion with creation and Creator. We might consider the ministry of St. Francis and the mendicants or the Benedictines in Iona who chose to live and work within harsh environments and are part of our deep Christian tradition and history. I have seen illustrated manuscripts that show monks praying outside and even reciting the psalms in a stream.

As such, practicing meditation outdoors, or even by an open window, enables the practitioner to be absorbed into the sonic backdrop of the natural context. Paying attention to these environmental soundscapes can then help to calibrate the mind into a mode of restful consciousness, where the jarring, dualistic separation between self and environment starts to blur. It can become a means of connecting with God as a mystery revealed through nature, of inhabiting and embracing an existential landscape, where one's sense of belonging is intensified and peace can be readily cultivated. My mother gave me *Walden* by Henry David

Thoreau (1854, 1995) when I was thirteen. Ever since, I have thought of environments and their soundscapes as sacred revelatory spaces.

One of my earliest prayer experiences was learning the practice of environmental soundscapes at a beautiful place called Camp Allen. It is the Episcopal Church camp where I ministered for many years. I grew to love how meditation, enveloped by God's creation, had a particular and unique feeling compared to the oneness experienced in church. What I learned in that sacred environment is a practice that can travel with me wherever I find myself.

For the neurodivergent, several sensory-sensitive approaches to meditation can be important to consider. The neurodivergent can include those with autism, those with attention deficit disorder (ADD), those with sensory processing disorders, or those with some other neurological variation. A loud room or a room with a strong fragrance can be uncomfortable.

To create a sensory-sensitivity-friendly environment, consider what can be tailored to an individual's needs to make for a more comfortable practice. This might mean using low, soft lighting or lowering the lights entirely. It can also include having noise-canceling headphones or ambient noise (to lower outside stimulation while using white or pink noise for focus) or playing soft, ambient sounds (such as nature sounds) along with meditation. This can extend to weighted blankets. Creating a space that feels safe to the individual by eliminating distractions, limiting external stimuli, and reducing sensory overload can be extraordinarily useful for enjoying and accruing the benefits of restful meditation (Kabat-Zinn, 1990).

Since many neurodivergent people, including those with ADD, can find it difficult to manage stillness, meditation practices can be modified to include movement. Walking meditation or stretching, with or without yoga, might be a more accessible alternative to the seated approach to meditation. These movements keep the body grounded and reduce discomfort and restlessness (Nhất Hạnh, 1991). Rocking and pacing are other ways of moving the body in sync with breathing, such as when repetitive motions or foot tapping help maintain one's grounding in meditation. Imagine here the ancient prayer practice of the faithful Jews at the wailing wall in Jerusalem. This is called *shuckling*, in Yiddish, and dates from the eighth century.

One of the strengths commonly cited in neurodivergent individuals, especially those on the autism spectrum, is an ability to hyperfocus on those areas of intense interest. This talent can be leveraged in the form of meditation and contemplation.

I see meditation tools like this being used in one of our congregations in Texas called St. Andrews in the Heights, Houston. On Sunday afternoons, they have a service called Rhythms of Grace, created by Lisa Puccio. This worship service uses many of the prayer types just mentioned to create a worship space for all bodies. I have had profound spiritual experiences myself in these services. As a bishop, I also am asked to pray for them. We call it confirmation in my tradition, where I lay hands on a person's head or hold their hands and pray that they may continue God's forever and daily increase in God's spirit more and more until they come to rest in God's heavenly kingdom. This is not merely prayer but a physical act of prayer. Every body is worthy of prayer and every body may offer prayers worthy of God's love.

Structure and predictability are helpful building blocks for many neurodivergent people, providing a framework for engagement that enables them to hold the structure in working memory and engage in contemplation. This could include practicing formal meditation at a set time each day and structuring it with a sequence of individual actions and specified tools intended to concentrate the mind (the sound of a bell is one example). Such structure can lessen anxiety and provide a safe space to enter meditation.

All embodied beings can practice spiritual resistance. We return to where we started, remembering that the power of our spiritual practices comes from differences, not similarities. Every body, whatever ability, whatever sensory experience, whatever cognitive difference, can participate in powerful, spiritual forms of resistance. In embracing this diversity, we resist ableist and exclusionary norms around meditation that attempt to neatly sort people into bodies deemed capable.

When we deliberately make space and provide practices attentive to all bodies, we provide access points to the holy, spiritual, and embodied resistance. Silence and stillness are understood not as dormant but as active states of resistance; they are not invisible patterns but living spaces ready for the work of reclamation of ourselves and others—just as movement and sound are not disturbances but may also be forms of prayer.

Chapter Five

The Temptation of Modern Spiritualism

Resistance: Gathering in Community

Our bodies, too, like Christ's body, are holy and indivisible from our souls, and this is a direct challenge to the digital's insistent disembodiment of spirit from flesh. The most authentic form of resistance is the liturgical, the embodied, the community.

—A. D.

The Body

Saint Paul's letters include expansive theological language, and he uses the body metaphor as a key to this understanding of the importance of the diverse people of the faith. Paul provided for Christians, especially those in my tradition, an understanding that *all* means *all*. Consider Paul's words to one community: "There is no longer Jew or Greek; there is no longer slave or free; there is no longer male and female, for all of you are one in Christ Jesus" (Galatians 3:28–29). Alternatively, in Paul's passages regarding Christ's love he is arguing that God's love is meant for all people so as to make everyone a member of God's Abrahamic covenant (Romans 4:13–18); and his passage about how nothing can separate us from God's love, not even powers or principalities (Romans 8:38–39). Moreover, this vision of Christ, his love, and our love for all others is essential (1 Corinthians 13:1–13).

Paul understood that Christ had come for all people. The crux of Paul's teaching is the unity of our body and the corporate body; these are important theological and spiritual revelations about God and God's creation. In the passages from several letters, Paul reminds us of our body's human unity and corporate unity under Christ's love and grace (Ephesians 1:22–23, Colossians 1:18, and Ephesians 5:23–24).

Paul wrote in these passages that we are the work of God's creation. He says the body is one, even though we know it has different parts. The Spirit of God provides, for each part of the body, its dignity. Paul says this is true of Christ as well. The mystery of Christ, this corporeal Jesus, is one, just like all bodies. Then he reminds us that we are all part of this relationship and that baptism is the primary way we outwardly recognize this truth in Christianity. We are united in our bodies by Christ's body and the spirit of God. This is a unifying theological way of speaking, and ultimately it is about our unity with God.

Paul, after speaking about the unity of our bodies and the unity of Christ's body, moves to offer this as a metaphor for humanity: he points out that one part of our body cannot say, "You are not part of us," or another say, "I no longer need you." This is not to describe "perfect" bodies but to point out what he knew before the modern age—the body is one.

Paul then goes further to say that there are reasons why the entire body is not an eye or a nose. We could just as quickly say that the whole body is not only a brain. He says the wholeness of the body is essential, and if one part is hurt, the rest of the body suffers. He concludes by saying this is what it is like to be a body of people.

In these two pieces of Paul's overall essential teachings, we understand the importance of the unity of the human body and the body of humans. This is wise and helpful to our discussion because, in our present technological culture and constant connectivity, we have deconstructed the care for human bodies and divided ourselves as human beings from each other. Here, I find theological truth from Paul about God and Jesus, about ourselves, that I can hold as I step into a contrary theology of resistance.

Christ's conception and birth in the flesh are not some accidental wrinkles of Christian thought. They are the foundation of Christianity upon which the theology of the cross and resurrection are built. The coming in the flesh of Christ announces that the material body is not something evil, but instead that the body is a worthy vessel of God. For me, the death of Christ upon the cross in full fleshiness is at the core of our tradition regarding the human body. Here, we express Jesus's whole bodily mystery, which incorporates into his life and death the reality of a finite body that bleeds, suffers, and dies.

Paul reminds us that not one part of the body can suffer without the other parts participating. In the bodily nature of God's Incarnation and cross, we are then able to see our own deep connection with Christ and those who suffer in any way or are oppressed. We understand God's love that connects us physically to each other. In this truth, we also come to terms with the reality that suffering is part of the human experience, and it is what it means to share a body and be a part of a corporate body of people. We are then metaphysically connected to God in Jesus's body and each other's body.

Here is the core of an unabashed faith: Jesus's body was the same as ours, and our body then is the same as Jesus's. This truth unites us individually and corporately, and nothing can separate us from this fact of created union. Moreover, by sharing this unabashed faith, we denounce the possibility that there is only good or bad, body or spirit, God separate from humanity and creation. In this faith, we recognize that technology, no matter how it seems, is only made up of manipulated matter from natural resources and thus does not have flesh and so cannot be inhabited by spirit. An unabashed faith rejects that there can be a ghost in the machine and that robots dream of sheep (see Philip K. Dick's *Do Androids Dream of Electric Sheep?*). For Christians, our theology supports the idea that God's spirit is present in aliens more than it might support the idea that God's spirit will be found in our robot friends.

Dualism locates spirit and body on mutually exclusive planes of good and evil. God's whole narrative heralds another option: what is material and what is spirit are not radically opposed but rather intrinsically related. The body is not the tomb but the temple of the soul. It is in the flesh that we live. It is in the flesh that we love. We can only understand Christ's body through our bodies. We partake of the divine not through denying the world but by accepting every body and creation. Furthermore, in knowing ourselves to be human bodies, we become more Christlike. In seeking to be more Christlike, we become more bodily human.

The mystery of Jesus was not an illusion. Jesus did live. He was crucified, died, and rose again for the life of the whole world and all creatures. His presence was stamped into creation and its matter, its fleshiness. Christ crucified was not only a spiritual sacrifice but a bodily one: the pouring-out of the fullness of the strength itself of our humanity; thus, Christ's rising was not merely his victory over the grave—it is our future victory.

In assuming flesh, Christ has irrevocably yoked together the divine and the human, the spiritual and the material, heaven and earth, all the matter and that which is in-between and can never be undone (an eschatological union).

Therefore, redefined by Christ, the body is no longer an enemy of God and the adversary of the spiritual good; embodied life is no longer a source of shame and radical alienation from the spiritual life. This theology proclaims that the body is a means toward faith, able to return to creation as a cooperating instrument in God's renewal and redemption.

In a more popular language metaphor, we would say we reject the notion that our bodies are living life as a "meat puppet"—a living host that a puppeteer has taken control of. Neither are we shells overtaken by a parasite that turns us into zombies, nor inhabited by a body snatcher, nor similar science fiction or horror trope. We are not playthings of fate or the divine; we are not doing the will of an alien puppeteer from the sky. These are all examples of popular science fiction and horror within our context. However, they are important because they highlight within our popular literature and film the fear of dualism and the separation of the body from the spirit. These tropes point toward the real bodily experience and understanding that something is not right in our shared common anxiety.

We are still awaiting the perfection of the worldly body. With Christ, we shall in the end all be judged worthy of the fullness of the resurrection, as our own body will have fully and gloriously realized the image of the heavenly body. I want you to understand that an unabashed faith announces the lie of a transcendence that ends and escapes the materiality of the flesh. An unabashed faith announces the body's transformation, for it is in and through our flesh that we are met by Christ, who for our sake took on our substance, that we might share his (Philippians 2:7–9). What is good in creation has come to us, and what is redeeming (the good news of the body) is now a gift to be claimed. We see in this unabashed faith that the fruit of the Tree of Knowledge is not the whole story. Everything is not as the human body seems to understand it. It is, in fact, only here on Earth that we can taste and see the goodness of the body of the mystery of the Lord (Psalm 91). Furthermore, we can only partially know this goodness (1 Corinthians 13:12).

The Nature of Digital Disembodiment

As our digital age evolves, increasingly face-to-screen rather than face-to-face, something is lost. We have been disembodied. An unabashed faith in our humanity comes from our physicality, our embodied being. Our bodiless selfies, our relationship with people through screens, our realities communicated through data, and the inundation of pixels over daily perceptual experience all contribute to that Babylonian captivation. It is physically exhausting our bodies. I call this "aesthetic pollution." It characterizes digital culture within a media-saturated environment where the aesthetic beauty of God is polluted.

In his book *The End of Absence,* Michael Harris is convinced the antidote to what ails us is that, as human beings, we need to talk with each other. He believes that we have lost something by not being in conversation in real life (Harris, 2015). As I have pointed out in the research, the cure for lonesomeness is embodied gatherings of people who speak to each other. We know through reading that early technologies—particularly automatons or ventriloquist machines—were created by humans to captivate humans. It is as if we are stuck in the movie *Big* (1988) with Tom Hanks, and we cannot find the automaton ventriloquist machine that grants him a wish. And, when he wants out of the wish, the machine is nowhere to be seen.

French philosopher Gilbert Simondon calls this beguilement of the human mind an "operational fetishism" (Simondon, 2007). He believes that humans must take this mode of existence seriously to create a more ethical future where mechanical objects continue to evolve. Simondon goes a step farther and articulates a mode of existence for technological objects as he seeks to articular our human relationship with machines (Simondon, 2017). He believes that humans must take this mode of existence seriously to create a more ethical future where mechanical objects continue to evolve lest we be entranced by them.

Another French philosopher, Jean-Luc Marion, discusses a "bodiless gaze" in which we see the other's image but not the embodied spirit. We can see the "outsides" but not comprehend the "insides." Our body receives data and information but not the wholeness of the other human being. In his book *The Crossing of the Invisible,* Marion suggests that when the consumer connects visually, the human being can be saturated and overwhelmed. Our bodies limit what we take in so as not to overwhelm us. We do not fully experience the phenomenological nature of objects; for example, we cannot fully experience the phenomenon of the entangled body and spirit of another human being (Marion, 2020).

I suggest that what we learn from Simondon and Marion is that we are addicted to and cannot possibly comprehend the fullness of the constant bodily bombardment of technology, data, and information. We are addicted to the fetishism of technology but cannot see the addiction. We feel anxious, so we consume prescription drugs to help ourselves deal with the anxiety while at the same time continuing to place ourselves into a life overwhelmed by the sensual constant connectivity that can cause anxiety.

French sociologist Jacques Ellul wrote a philosophical and theological critique of technology in *The Technological Society* (1964). He claims that the more technology advances and permeates human life, the more it estranges human beings from their corporeality and nature and from anything that remains authentic. He makes a similar argument as Jean Baudrillard makes in *Simulacra and Simulation* regarding the multiplication of images and objects that move away from the original and, as they do, lose their reality (Baudrillard, 1994). For Baudrillard, the genuine and authentic lose their nature as they are replicated and reproduced in the world of mass production and mass data. Everything becomes a hollow, disembodied replica of itself. I argue that our bodies shift toward meaninglessness and disconnection as we become poor physical representations of our online projection of ourselves. Consider Jürgen Habermas's point that we are reduced as humans to "instrumental agents": creatures integrated into a web of interlocking systems so that we are dematerialized into the machinery of those systems themselves (Yates, 2021).

Austrian theologian and priest Ivan Illich offers a corrective idea: what he calls "conviviality," a friendliness that resumes human beings' free and creative relationships between themselves and their surroundings (Illich, 1975). He sees life becoming subject to a radical monopoly in which digital mediation increasingly replaces all other modes of relating, including religious life. This digital mediation replaces embodied relationships in flesh and blood. The derivatization, as he calls it, or disembodiment of the human person, is starkly honest about where we are today.

Disembodied IoT and Spiritualism

In an age of disconnection and disembodiment, we see a rise in theologies that remove the spirit from embodiment and seek to separate consciousness from the body itself. We also see a rise in what might be called a new spiritualism. The continuing possibility of disembodiment through technology and spiritualism is a mixture that will have some influential voices in the coming future, yet I am offering something different in this book.

Spiritualism has been part of the human desire for divine connection for thousands of years. We are in the age of new spiritualism, which is not the same as Christian spirituality. This is an important topic because when contemplation and meditation are discussed as a form of prayer and unity with the divine, spiritualism is not addressed as a practice. Spiritualists believe they can communicate by employing a medium with the supernatural and can communicate with the spirits of deceased persons. This speaks to the idea that our souls are free from our bodies—from embodiment. This new spiritualism is a partner for the IoT age because it, too, focuses on a nonconnected body and mind or spirit. Spiritualism is dualistic.

Tarot cards are employed as prophetic signage in spiritualism and will lead you down a dualistic path. There is renewed interest in using tarot cards within Christian spiritual practice. Such cards seek to tell a person's future path using divination, which is not the same as contemplation or meditation on God. Note that Christianity does not believe in telling the future. The present moment is not the first time that Christians have tried or used this practice. Time and again the church has responded that this is not part of our belief system.

Today, the most used tarot deck dates to 1910, even though the practice of using them for divination first emerged around 1480. The "Rider-Waite Deck," popularized by its creators, Pamela Colman and Arthur Edward Waite, became famous for its symbols, colors, and suits of kings, queens, jacks, and knights instead of spades, hearts, clubs, and diamonds. One performs a tarot reading by shuffling and cutting the cards and then expending them in a spread, like the Celtic cross or the Past, Present, Future, and Love cards. From here, the tarot card is seen as behaving like a window to the soul. Practitioners say it must be read by the user looking into themselves, on account of the cards' operating on a higher plane of existence, to which the vagaries of physicality hinder the ability to peer. (My grandmother used to dress up and read fortunes for people. As a child, I was jealous because she would not read the cards for family members. But this is how I knew what they are.)

In Christianity, such cards are used to discern the divine will for you and your future. The problem is that the church (all churches) has stated clearly in creed and confession that our future is provided to us by God and Christ, that scripture is not a divining tool but the living Word of God, and that sacraments are vessels of grace and healing for sacramental churches.

Throughout time, people have looked to astrology, which is the study of the constellations and their influence on humans, animals, and nature based on the positions and alignments of the stars. The system was created by the ancient Babylonians and Chaldeans sometime near 3,000 BCE (Before the Common Era). Later, the Ancient Greeks refined the concept and divided the twelve constellations into 30-degree quadrants. People use it today to understand the influence of the movement of planets on their lives. People may even read astrology charts, which help a person make decisions correctly and analyze historical events. While astrology is mentioned in the scriptures, it is not a means to listen to God. Several texts remind us that these signs are not signs of revelation (Matthew 16:2; Acts 1:7; and I Thessalonians 5:1–11). Astrology is not part of the Christian tradition in part because, in my tradition, we believe in science. However, astrology as a tool for spiritualism speaks of the unseen forces of the universe's effect upon your spirit.

Another part of spiritualism is automatic writing. It is seen as a form of psychical research in which the medium, while fully awake or in a trance state, writes divinely inspired messages that reveal hidden knowledge of the universe and, in some instances, associated drawings or images. In this way, the body becomes a pass-through for another spirit's inhabitation or communication. The spirit is again disembodied here.

People today use runes. Runes are a series of letters recovered from ancient burial sites in Northern Europe and placed upon a bone or stone. They are stones written with spellings (letters) that may carry meaning: twenty-four runes represent the twenty-four what-ifs of the world. Like how ancient Bantu people used bones, coins, or shells to divine the future, spell a word, or influence a situation, practitioners believe runes summon knowledge and energy when thrown. Here an object or tool is used to divine the future for the spirit.

Scrying, or gazing, is the wizard's, witch's, or soothsayer's attempt to receive clairvoyant insights via reflections on highly polished paraboloids (including crystal balls, water, glass, and mirrors). Here, one believes they are staring through the reflecting surface and into another plane of existence. This is different than the Christian use of an icon. The point of the icon is not to transfer into another plane or to see another plane. Instead, an icon provides a means for calming the mind from the bombardment of images and to settle into a direct relationship between the body and the divine.

Some people use crystals as part of their practice of spiritualism. These stones are believed to be infused with energy, which affects the subconscious mind and emotions, and can be used in divination healing rituals and meditation. Set in jewelry, they are said to portray each day of the year and, thus, help to guide one's existence. Crystals are often accompanied by other occult practices, such as tarot, astrology, and runes. Practitioners believe they exert a healing power on individuals by purifying and shielding them from evil spells. Here, though, the Christian believes that God's love provides ultimate deliverance from suffering. In my tradition, when we lay hands upon someone for prayers, we remind them of God's love and invite them to trust that evil, death, and suffering will not have the last word. It is not my laying on of hands or the oil that protects them. These are signs of their bodily relationship with God.

Some spiritualist readers use the art of reading herbs, tea leaves, and coffee grounds, interpreting patterns left in the remains of a cup after the beverage has been consumed. Herbs and plants are also used in ritual practices to ward off evil energies. Believers use dowsing and a pendulum in similar ways. This is a belief that people can control natural things to provide the power of deliverance.

The communication with spirits without bodies is central to spiritualism. Spiritualism became popular after the death of so many in World War I when the global society powerfully felt loss. It was a way of seeking to heal an unmet grief of the world's suffering people. The people of the world are grieving now for loved ones who died during COVID-19. There is no return to normal after losing more than 7,064,380 million people and rising (World Health Organization, n.d.). This is significantly less than the estimated 40-plus million who died during World War I. However, I would suggest the loss of our communities, the loss of religion, the loss of connectivity with other human beings, the loneliness and loss of so many people in the world today, plus an annual death toll of humans of around 60 million, is a powerful motivator for seeking answers and certainty. There is a cumulative loss being experienced by humanity.

This new spiritualism is rising in popularity because, in a world without religion itself, humans tend toward a super individualist understanding of the spirit/soul and, in so doing, suggest we are nothing but souls inhabiting a body for a short while. The second reason is that there are real questions about augmenting individuals who are no longer alive through artificial intelligence so that peoplc may be advised by them. Lastly, the new spiritualism seeks salvation through technology. This emerging technological project has had myriad conversations over the last thirty years on saving us. People have begun to speak about saving themselves in the machine. There are several examples, like Frank Tipler's *The Physics of Immortality* (1994) as just one example. Technology and spiritualism are founded upon a philosophy and theology of dualism.

Moreover, there is much dualism in today's Christianity. Let me say clearly that this is not the way of praying for the unabashed Christian. So, let me again reassert the importance of the body and how we have approached this in my Anglican and Episcopal traditions as an example.

Many of the theologians of my Christian tradition turn to St. Augustine of the fourth century, one of the most influential Church theologians who grappled with the nature of the human body as it relates to the soul, especially in the context of resurrection. I first read his corpus in seminary. Augustine rejected the notion of purely spiritual bodies, emphasizing that the resurrection involves the physical body, albeit transformed. For Augustine, the body is not something to be discarded or transcended in favor of a purely spiritual existence; instead, it is an essential part of human being-ness that will be changed in the resurrection. This view underscores the importance of the body in Christian theology, challenging dualistic notions that devalue the material world.

Augustine's thoughts on the resurrection align with a broader theological commitment to the goodness of creation. He argued that the resurrection of the body demonstrates God's power to redeem all of creation, not just the soul. This belief counters the idea that the material world is inherently corrupt or inferior to the spiritual realm. Instead, Augustine saw the body as integral to the person, destined to be glorified in the afterlife.

Philosophical Perspectives on Disembodiment

To understand the ramifications of digital disembodiment, we must turn to the philosophical tradition that has long been contemplating this essence of body-mind relations, its descriptions, and its implications as they relate to their entanglement with technology. Traditionally, no metaphysical line was drawn between the body and the mind; quite simply, they have been co-located entities in a bodily oneness.

In twentieth-century France, Maurice Merleau-Ponty argued in his book, *Phenomenology of Perception,* that the body is not merely a means or device of the mind to act upon the world; instead, all understanding unfolds through, and in light of, our bodies. He argued that knowledge is a structure forged between the embodied ways of being in the world. This suggests that any diminishment in the relation between body and mind—the fragmentation of their entanglement, such as uploading—impairs our capacity to understand the world. (Merleau-Ponty, 1994)

Jacques Ellul's core concept was technological alienation. He is dependent upon Merleau-Ponty's argument. He takes Merleau-Ponty's existentialist thinking further by showing how modern technology reinforces the concept of a mind's unhoused state. Ellul explains how the world is becoming more and more instrumentalized through the spread of technology, working to transform all our human experiences into instrumentalized interactions that narrowly reduce things down to mere transactions. In this way, the Internet of Things should be more aptly described as the Internet of Transactions. Following this argument, Ellul suggests that there will be many losses. Among them, technology sets us up for spiritual poverty—a new and subtler form of exile, from which life might seem catatonic, but culture becomes manic for it. By injecting the veins of our reality with digital serums of information exchange that push an objectifying and instrumental attitude, we feel more and more dispossessed from our bodies and one another (Ellul, 1964).

Illich argued that digital technologies have a de-skilling effect, further alienating individuals from their bodies and communities. In his book *Conviviality,* he describes modern technology as a preferred world where practices and tools are built with our bodies, communities, and humans flourishing in mind. In the world of conviviality, technology is a tool that complements or supplements but never supplants our physical and spiritual relation to the world and one another. We might ask if the tool of technology has been developed with conviviality and human flourishing in mind as opposed to the flourishing of particular individuals. Does technology reconnect us to the earth and dirt of creation? Is this an opportune moment to question if that might be an operating value beyond free markets and consumerism? (Illich, 1975).

Marion also addresses the problem of embodiment and analyzes idolatry in its modern manifestations. Marion aimed his critique at idolatry or *l'image,* i.e., the promotion of images over embodied experience (what one might term lived experience). We might think of the persistence of modern idolatry as idolatry exchanges or idolatry economics. In this context, the origins of univocity—this is his concept of bypassing the real in the human being through misdirected attention toward images—are exposed in the modern commoditized sense of the term. There is no guarantee that people will come together because of new technological developments, nor does it imply that political, economic, and social processes will work benignly. I know that a dualistic digital spirituality will create more distance: people, out of vanity and solipsism, create a disembodied world with virtual selfies (Marion via translation by Cavanaugh, 2024).

Theologians and philosophers have been fighting dualism since the third century through the Enlightenment, the Industrial Revolution, the emergence of technology in the 1960s, and today, with the birth of a new age. This notion of a separate spirit from the body and the use of machines has been around since the Industrial Revolution, within the last hundred-plus years, and a continuing prophetic vision of things to come in our time. Moreover, it is a moment to recognize that there is another way to find deliverance from those things that ail us.

The *Corpus Mysticum*

Thus, removing the body—the disembodiment of human exchange facilitated by digital technologies—was never just a social problem or a psychological issue. It was a problem of the spirit. The Roman Catholic philosopher Louis Pierre Althusser argued that we were being separated from each other. From the 1960s forward, he suggested we were being reshaped into individuals minus the meaning the individual used to have amidst the shared collective human beings. He called it digital demobilization. For Althusser, communal prayer was a way for a person to better understand one's body and that body amidst others and God. In line with many, including Paul, Althusser believed you cannot separate the body and soul from nature and what it means to be a human being. He believed these three aspects—physical, mental, and spiritual—were complementary and inseparable (Eldridge, 1993).

As digital technologies continue to demoralize human communion and diminish our awareness of humanity's unique physical, mental, and spiritual capacities, the gathering of the embodied for prayer (an embodied communal presence) represents the only means by which we might rehabilitate the awareness, the *cogito*, of the individual spirit's embeddedness in the body. The individual body requires the corporate body. By emphasizing the role of physicality in prayer, the turn to bodily gathering as a corrective also reinvigorates the communal aspect of the *corpus mysticum*—the mystical body of Christ. When you gather with others in prayer or meditation, something important is happening—something that cannot happen in solitude.

We must recover a fully embodied, integrated, and multisensory understanding of our life language. In the face of digital disembodiment, we must hold an unabashed faith in the nature of our bodies. In prayer and meditation, we can resist and reclaim that the embodied nature of the human person matters in ways worth pondering. Digital technologies can seek to dismantle embodied experience, flattening out our encounters into two-dimensional screens and digital avatars. Awareness of what we are resisting helps us focus on the importance of proximity and the presence of our bodies in the community.

Proximity and Presence in Gathering

The basic form of a gathering gives the ideas of nearness and presence concrete expression. Congregating a group of bodied people who believe in the mystery of Jesus Christ and the oneness of God and humanity is key to resisting anti-spiritual influences. No matter what your tradition is, Christian or not, gathering to meditate is resistance. Prayer draws us closer to God and to others. Monks of all religions have revealed this to be true. Not only is this a full-body experience for the individual, but it is also a corporate full-bodied reality.

The development of the digital age poses a real challenge to this essential requirement of an unabashed faith. With the accessibility of televised and internet services, online prayer groups, and digital ministry, there is a real temptation to imagine that virtual presence equates with physical presence. It does not. The digital domain can and should facilitate genuine worship but cannot replace it.

Resistance Recap: Gathering in Community

Over the years, I have been helped by gathering in the community for prayer: in all kinds of gatherings, from silent retreats to monastic retreats, prayer meetings with others, guided group prayer, prayer bead gatherings, and sung Taizé prayer gatherings. The centrality of the Eucharist in my tradition has meant we have forgotten many old ways of gathering to pray together, of entering into what Ivan Illich called the proximity of human beings. Individual prayer and meditation will draw you to others, yet the action of gathering proceeds from the prayer and leads to growing as a convivial community—a reality that Jesus called spiritual friendship (John 15:15).

For Illich, full human engagement and the free flourishing of spiritual life came through embodied, communal interaction. In the ritual context, this means prioritizing in-person assemblies as the best way of engaging all the senses and paradoxes of human existence by meditating together. Digital tools are mere adjuncts to the living body(s). The living assembly animates and what we call community is created, coexisting in in-between spaces (Illich, 1975).

Just as individuals can seek out space for themselves, groups can make sacred places sacred. It also means finding time and pulling time out of daily diaries to gather. House churches and missional communities are other ways people can gather together and pray, just as I did when I first learned meditation in an empty classroom among my orthodox prayer partners.

Coming together to pray in silence is powerful. It may allow a leader to help us to renew our focus on prayer if we become distracted. There is, in fact, a rhythm to prayer together, just as there is in individual prayer time. We become aware of the time and space we are sharing—the bodily space we are sharing. We also become aware of the space in-between us.

Gatherings are ways of resisting the gravitational suck of digital constancy. So, while serious challenges are inherent in digital disembodiment, we ultimately make the unabashed faith choice to gather in prayer and meditation together, with words and in silence. Those who pray and meditate alone are drawn to such corporate practices of prayer by the very nature of becoming more aware of others and the divine. By making conviviality a priority and by making more of an effort to share this wisdom that considers the relationship between embodiment and the fullness of the Christian life, the church may be able to recover embodied communities that celebrate our role as the Body of Christ. In the digital age, we might find ourselves turning to existential solitude more, but the reality of who we are physically makes us the Body of Christ.

Chapter Six

Revitalizing Life Together: A Call to Kinship

Resistance: Communal Prayer and Sacramental Life

Prayer, both in solitude and with others,
is a type of resistance that shatters the falsehood that digitally managed togetherness is the same as real-life experience.
Kinship communities are a visible sign against a disjointed and de-incarnated world.

—A. D.

Our fractured world has lost its sense of community. I believe that God calls his people who multiply God's blessing of kinship and shalom in the world. I believe we are called to incarnate, preserve, and multiply the blessings of shalom, love, and peace, one act and moment at a time. We are to do this across our lifespans. I have learned this over my years of ministry, and I have seen it enliven people who participate in prayer and meditation as a corporate body that we call Christ. As individual bodies, the smallest acts of resistance of love and peace resist evil and the darkness of hopelessness.

God invites us to see that we are already a kinship community. As we enter both individual times of contemplation and prayer and gathered meditation, we learn—not just believe—that we "no longer live as strangers to one another by the flesh," as Paul suggests in his letter to the Galatians (Galatians 5:15). This is a recognition of our shared belongingness, not based upon tribal identity in this world but rather upon God's very identity. We are given our identity just as God has raised us from the earth and given us life along with all other creatures (Genesis 1:30). We are formed as one body in a global kinship.

Being in Christ, we are also in one another. We recognize one another as kin, not by family resemblance, habitat, lifestyle, location, occupation, or interests. We do not see our neighbor—our brother or sister—as another race, nationality, or social status. In Christ, we are no longer separated by these distinctions, but rather see reflected to us one humanity that transcends those separations by which we are still wound together. Through God our neighbor is genuinely one with us; we share the dignity of being human in God's image. We are kin because we are bound by divine love of God. We therefore share the responsibility of the mutuality of care. For those of us called Christians, this entails an extraordinary commitment, as it necessarily involves being even more intimate and imitating God's calling of his human image into his likeness. Furthermore, we are called and invited to lead a life of pilgrimage together with our kin.

Our contemplation creates awareness of each person we discover in a relationship-filled life. Our kinship—achieved by becoming more aware of one another's life journeys—can become that same shalom—God's peace. The fullness of justice and reconciliation can be expressed in a life of true liberty, released from the bondage of dissecting the world around us. We have taught each other to differentiate across lines of societal demarcation. This forces us into either-or situations. It requires us to see each other as different. Think of the reality that there is only one human race, not a multiplicity of races. The Christians in my tradition do not define themselves by their differences but rather by their dignity in Christ. This provides the possibility of the people's holistic prayers being prayed together.

It does set us off into different directions together, however. It means we become aware of the issue of how difference works to separate, categorize, hurt, build wealth, take advantage of the poor, and keep people out. If we say we are all given the dignity of kinship we are then forced to ask why does my sibling, my brother, my sister, not have the same opportunities as I do? What sacrifices must I make to ensure they receive love and care, and are treated with equity and the same justice as others? Sometimes it may mean remembering that certain parts of our community are left out, mistreated, or killed because of who they are. Kinship places their burden upon our hearts in such a way that we cannot ignore it.

In its fullest expression, shalom represents the peace of God, whose embrace rejects settling for the brokenness of human existence, heals the wounded, and reconciles what is divided. The peace of Christ calls us to set right a world of injustice. By living out this peace, we do not receive shalom—we multiply it, spread it out, and deepen it and bring God's conception of justice into a palpable reality.

At the center of this lineage is love—the self-sacrificial love of Christ that urges us to serve, not to be served;

to give, not to receive. It is a love that is not passive or complacent but active, sacrificial, seeking out the good of others. Love is incarnated in our gatherings of prayer, in which everyone can live out their God-ordained potential to be valued and supported. In prayer and meditation we are being connected and so through this connection we are prepared to serve, multiplying goodness, peace, and blessings for others.

This love is multiplied and shared first in an unabashed prayer between an individual and the divine. Then, it is given greater life by gathering people in prayer, quiet, and meditation. Here it begins to multiply. Then, throughout our daily walk through life we see opportunities because instead of the distraction of constant connectivity we will see the people before us. We will see in them who they are and not a person in my way, bothering me or interrupting me. This means that this work creates a firmly rooted body in the world. We take the first steps outside of our zombie life. We discover in time that we are no longer mindlessly present amidst other invisible humans, whose minds are shrouded by an invisible wall, diminished by our mutual acceptance of dualism and the body's unimportance. Now, we have become kin to those in front of us and with whom we interact. Our beginning in prayer multiplies as we live lives of intentionality.

When we become attentive to a life lived with God, we find that our response to kinship becomes a possibility. If God is love and peace, how can we not become love and peace in the world, after a visit in prayer? How can we not learn to love those we pray for to the God who is love? Sometimes our prayers are filled with acts of petition—asking God for this and for that. Certainly, praying for someone is important. And yet when we sit with God, we may lift them into God's presence. Think of petition where we close our eyes and take our friend who has cancer and is in hospice with us, seeing their face, their room, their bed. We lift this image to God and pray for peace and allow peace to be present. In this way we are praying for them and we are being changed. Our bodies receive peace too at the loss of a friend. We are reminded that this is not the end. We are able to literally hold them in prayer. This is both an attentive and intentional prayer of petition. In this way our life of prayer moves beyond a list of petitions to a deeper life of peace for us and the sake of all those in our life and community who desperately need our prayer and God's peace.

Here we are beginning to imagine together a life of wholeness and flourishing. Nevertheless, such a life will always be just beyond us if we only pray alone and go about the busyness of life alone. Love and peace, wholeness and flourishing, require friends. Kinship with God always leads us to kinship with others.

Resistance Recap: Community and Sacramental Life

God reminds us that being alone is not suitable for human bodies (Genesis 2:18). The one thing that cannot be shaken in Christian theology, as far as I can see, is the thrust of the divine revelation that we are to be together and to build community life together from the apostles' community, as they "devoted themselves to the apostles' teaching and fellowship, to the breaking of bread and prayer" in Acts 2:42; and Paul's metaphor of the Body of Christ where in fact God has placed the parts, every one of them, just as God wanted in 1 Corinthians 12:12–27. We have just talked about our kinship; indeed, there is a familial quality of a company of believers who regularly pray and meditate together. Gatherings are a key theme woven throughout the whole of the New Testament.

To pray together as kin is to begin to dwell together in a new and different way. There is accountability to one another, loving one another, and serving one another when we pray together and when we share and meditate together. I have found that in a profound way, when people pray together, they become aware of the burdens of others, even when words are not spoken. Here, we have some insight into a language of prayer that happens in the in-between. In a community, for example, one believer "bears one another's burdens" (Galatians 6:2).

When we are together, our prayer is a spiritual gift to one another, fostering unity among the company gathered. The greatest thing we can do to bind us together is pray with one another—whether that prayer is silent or with sound (Ephesians 4:11–16). An unabashed faith is a communal faith. Protestant theologian Dietrich Bonhoeffer suggested there is a difference between a spiritual community of prayer and a community connected by emotion (Bonhoeffer, 2015). Human beings are very susceptible to feelings in groups. Theologians long before Bonhoeffer knew this. American theologian and pastor Jonathan Edwards (1703-1758) was concerned with a Christianity that was unified by feeling only and said that there must be a knowing as well. German theologian Friedrich Schleiermacher (1768-1834) was also concerned about feelings only; his contribution was to add doing to feeling and knowing. To feel alone is to move into the realm of the spirit only, and it is also to be susceptible to crowd feelings. This is one of the problems that people face today when it comes to every kind of religion. They trust their feelings and so gravitate away from thoughts and actions that may make them uncomfortable.

After Bonhoeffer's time spent in Harlem during its Renaissance, he became aware of how important this prayer of a whole community drew people toward caring for others out of the most profound sense of God's love and identity with the lost (Williams, 2021). It was in a community filled with embodied spirit that sought to understand, to know, and to bring forth an identity that resisted the identity of racist America at the time. Their doing was the act of art and music, preaching, teaching, and creativity. Most of all it was a community that understood theologically that all embodied people regardless of the color of their skin were God's. Bonhoeffer understood God desired people's freedom from the powers that oppressed them by trying to convince the culture that oppressors were not human but rather brutes and beasts. In the Harlem Renaissance, Bonhoeffer heard the voice of God, which stirred him to comprehend that there was no white German "volk." Key to us today is that one of the important revelations, as we go deeper into white supremacist Nazis theology, is the idea that the Nazis believed they were the only ones who were God's people—it was a particularly nasty form of Christian nationalism. Bonhoeffer, after his experience of the Harlem Renaissance, understood this and the tragedy facing the Jews, and he felt called to action. Once he prayed in community, especially with a community of people finding their voice, he knew he could no longer avoid acting. He had to do something. Connecting in the act of worship and prayer brought about a connectivity between Bonhoeffer and all people that he had not felt before.

Sacramentality of Life

In the previous chapter on dualism and disembodied spirit I spoke of several sacraments from my Christian tradition. I spoke about the laying on of hands. I have also spoken about the Lord's supper and baptism. These are called sacraments in the Episcopal Church. Sacraments are signs that some Christians participate in that help connect them to each other and to God. Most are done with others, and some are done between a priest and the person who requests them. Some other Protestant denominations might consider the Bible a kind of sacrament, as reading it and praying it brings a sense understanding or grace. Sacraments are an act, accompanied by a sign, that speaks to God's grace, love, and peace given to each person. Therefore, a sacramental life is one that separates out time beyond private prayer in which people come together to pray; and they do so on a regular basis.

Social critic and philosopher Ivan Illich was deeply moved by the sacramental life of the community, as well as insightful about how institutions, modernity, and technology often destroy, degrade, or deform this idea, both in theory and in practice. Illich's thoughts about sacramentality are scattered throughout the corpus of his writing but are most explicitly developed in his critiques of institutionalized religion, schooling, and modern healthcare (Cayley et al., 2015).

Taking Illich's idea further, sacramental life is being appropriated by technology. Humankind, for ages, has built altars and found a deep sense of belonging and communing. Today, anti-spiritual forces like technology are slowly suppressing the body's sense of being connected to the sacred. As we have seen, it does this by providing an artificial form of bodily connection. Illich states that no organization (not even a church) can fully institutionalize sacramentality because of the inability to a) control the divine; b) control the access of people to the divine; and c) control the access of people to other people. No organization can truly control our bodily real-world connectivity. Living sacramentally will always be done amid creation and with other bodies, just as Christ did in the mystery of Jesus's body (Illich, 1991). We are not buffered human beings. When together we are constantly communicating with each other—even when we are silent.

I met Arnold recently when he checked me into a hotel. I was saying thank you and being grateful for his help with a complicated process. He told me he recently went to a hotel in another country where he signed in via his credit card and a key was dropped from a machine. There was no person. Then he told me he guessed that his job was at stake. I said, "Arnold, thank you for being here. I appreciate you and I am glad to meet you." We must see each other in real life and not pass each other by. A deeper understanding through community and the communal practice of hospitality helps us reflect back an embodied social generosity. Compassion for each other cannot be replicated in a professional technological or expedient atmosphere of exchange. Compassion is always an act that happens between bodies. Christianity has forever provided compassionate care for the sick and poor as a demonstration of our connectedness to the divine (Illich, 1976).

If you read Ivan Illich, Richard Rohr, Brian McLaren, or Cynthia Bourgeault—or sit with them—you will find that they believe, as I do, that the very act of contemplative and meditative prayer is at the heart of resistance in daily life. A life of prayer as individuals and prayer in the community is a life of resistance to the disembodied forces of technology. The very act of slowing time is an act of a sacramental life of resistance. A meal shared at a table or wherever we may be is a tool of conviviality that resists the encroachment of the alternative or altered reality of technology.

When we gather in prayer, we are making sacramental life present in the world. Moreover, life in the community (especially the life of the sacramental church) pushes back the front lines of the invasion of constant technological connectivity. It is a way of saying that there are sanctifying powers in this world that make the body's experience of the divine different.

At the very core of this lived life of prayer in community is a reclamation of what is true about the in-between. There is a power to embodied community.

Sacramentality and Prayer in Worship

Sacramental prayer has a profoundly spiritual nature. David Bentley Hart emphasizes this idea: the sacramental life itself serves to gain one entrance into the life of God as an unending and infinite community. These ideas run like threads throughout Hart's body of work. He has written and been asked to write numerous times about these matters: the sacramental life, the nature of the Church, and the eschatological vision of Christian life.

Participation in Divine Reality

Hart captures my imagination as he speaks of the sacramental life of prayer, where our human bodies participate in the infinite reality of the divine life. Like Saint John of the Cross, a Christian Spanish contemplative, Hart does not speak of this as a mind experience but rather as a whole body experience. The actions of sacramental life are not simply a ritual action of symbolism. Hart, like many others, has helped me think of sacramental life, most notably in the Eucharist, as an encounter. That is how we must think about this—an encounter in which we must open our bodies to receive it. The Eucharist is something that takes place within us. St. Augustine suggests we are made for this: a deep, bodily place hungry just for this encounter that Hart suggests is rooted in that which is beyond us; it is the transcendent, open to the breaking in of an infinite encounter through a finite body. This is not limited to the elements of bread and wine; a whole church service can be a contemplative communion with the Trinity. By the Trinity, Hart means body, spirit, and the great mystery of God, which are present for us (Hart, 2004). Here is the mystery of Jesus confronted in community form, different and the same as the one whom we connect with through individual meditation.

The Eucharist as Infinite Communion

A young woman once told her priest that when she experiences the communion table in worship, she feels as though she is at the end of the table of Jesus, and all around, those who have gone before and after are gathered. In such a simple way, she has spoken of what Hart calls the bodily encounter at the table of the infinite. We are in his theological understanding of sacraments, participating in the infinite, eternal community of communion that he deems our proper destiny, both now and in the world to come.

In my tradition, we think of table fellowship in many ways, mostly about receiving something. The whole point is to get the wine and bread. This was revealed in the time of COVID-19. One priest told me how a person pressed past them after the service, where there was no sacrament, went to the ambry (that place where wine and bread are held), and took the sacrament himself. The life of sacramental prayer is not a solo experience between a person and God but rather a whole experience of all the people together. In our gathering, something mysterious and divine happens amongst us.

During the service at the table, we are at once remembering the past (it is a memorial action) and at the same time that which awaits us at our end. We are at the table with God, who is alpha and omega. I think that we break spiritually through our present body and liturgy into a space so slowed that we can be mindful of the presence of God and all that is past, and all that is to come. St. Augustine helps me here by considering time in his book *Confessions*, which is still one of my favorite books by him (Augustine, 2017). I believe an unabashed faith engages in deep resistance to see the present moment and refutes the technology's notion that we are the center of the eucharistic event. Instead, a sacramental life is much more than becoming present in a slower moment. Augustine would say there is no past and no future but only our experience of the present moment in time. Therefore, in contemplation, meditation, and shared prayer we experience together what Augustine called the past present, the present, and the present future, all at once. In the mystery of the Eucharist, the Christian church uniquely and most fully participates in God's divine life; moreover, the Eucharist anticipates a future reconciliation of all things *πanta*, meaning we experience all through God (Hart, 2011).

Sacramental Life: The Cosmic Scope of Resistance

The world is a place that barters fear in exchange for salvation promises. If you get enough likes, you will be an influencer; if you share this, you will be famous. Think about how much the economic commodification of self-worth is essential to a free market. This can be no less present in a church that has succumbed to a promise of salvation if you do this or that right. The past moralities that have upheld power inside and outside of the church are very real.

Participating in prayer and sacramental life is to receive in the depth of its meaning an experience through a particular instrument (bread, wine, water, and oil) of God's cosmic love, extending throughout the universe. This space in between us and these elements, these words, and even in between the silent breaths of the person at prayer points to the great mystery of prayer communities (specifically through the church) in which our paths of grace crisscross amidst life in God and God's creation.

Far from being about God only, elements only, or bodies only, the sacramental life participates in a love beyond us. This is partly why the individual nature of meditation and participation in group prayer and sacramental life draw us out of ourselves toward others (Hart, 2021).

The Church as a Sacramental Community

The church, at its best, becomes a group of gathered people at prayer, which then can be recognized as a type of sacramental community. This very presence of prayer and sacrament in the world is a vision of the heart of Christ in Paul's metaphor. We can see that participation shows a type of bodily reunion with God. The theological metaphor of church and body and the mystery of Jesus represents a powerful witness of God's continued sacramental life among us. Hart's theological understanding of this union between the divine and the body always points to our communal destiny as members of God's fellowship of love.

Sacraments Configure Life

Theologian Rowan Williams writes that if you want to understand what sacraments do, look at how the Christian community is formed structurally; the sacraments have something to do with the configuration of a particular church and a certain group of people in a specific place and at a particular time.

He suggests that the sacraments give life and identity to the gathered. This is a radical thought of resistance, for it indicates that this configuration of communal life also creates a configuration in our human life. The possibility of practiced sacramental life has a greater influence upon your body's well-being than does your constant connectivity with technology for the rest of your life. It is not our life that gives meaning to the sacraments, but God's body in Christ that provides the configuration and meaning. Here is the structure that Williams is talking about.

Williams articulates well that we become part of the reality of Christ's body through the sacraments. He characterizes the sacramental life as the realization that makes the Church the Body—made one with Christ in death and then raised again—and, simultaneously, that the Body is designed to be a witness in the world (Williams, 2014). Baptism, Eucharist, Confirmation, healing prayers, forgiveness, and prayers at death are ways of marking life with sacramental prayer.

Williams points to baptism as the root sacrament and sacramental experience that marks Christians as members of the Body of Christ. Baptism is not just a rite of passage or a ritual of initiation, but instead one of transformation. Through baptism, believers are marked as part of the people of God; through Christ and his body, their baptismal identity is knit into the world within the Christian community. Baptism inaugurates a pattern of sacramental activity that becomes part of the believer's life as a sustainable practice within the Christian Church. For the person and the world, it reminds us that bodies are essential, as is an embodied theology.

Cynthia Bourgeault writes about the sacramental prayer life and suggests the work of prayer is a particularly and uniquely profound incarnational practice. In other words, this is about our body and the mystery of Jesus's body. She emphasizes centering prayer and prayer with the divine as dialogue. For a moment, let us remember our thoughts from previous chapters, as she emphasizes this type of prayer as falling away amidst a receptive space both within and without the body. The centering prayer for her is to rid the body of an accepted but not true dualistic consciousness (Bourgeault, 2016). For her, there is an enfolding of awareness. She might say we make room in the world and within our bodies for the divine.

Sacramental prayer for Bourgeault is not a transaction but a ritual action of prayer that is acted out by the sacred. For the body, this dynamic engagement draws the whole embodied person into a sacramental river (Page & Bourgeault, 2013). During sacramental life, we are drawn into the divine mystery individually and corporately. For example, the body is given a new memory of life with a loving God.

I have contemplated Bourgeault's wisdom that we are not imitating something as a metaphor. As Baudrillard points out in his philosophy, we are not simply participating in a remaking repeatedly as if it were kitsch so far removed from its original—and not in a good way. We are not conforming to a ritual action long separated from its meaning. This takes some work on the part of the body, which I will talk about at the end of this chapter, as it is practicing sacramental participation. The ritual of participating together as gathered bodies intentionally with the divine is not a dualism between material and spiritual, sharing similar space in the hopes that something might happen. Prayer together is a practice.

I remember Bourgeault once saying in a gathering something like: The sacramental prayer life reorients our experience to a bodily experience of God's presence in the world. We begin to see the world differently and comprehend that our lives, the lives of other bodies, and the lives of the world are imbued with sacrality—with sacred significance.

In addition, such an idea of the sacramental life of prayer taps into Jesus's words from scripture that we are in the world but different (John 17:14–15). We are in the world but not in the oppressive systems of powers and principalities. We see things from a different angle. It is as if we are, through the practice of prayer both individually and together, trained to see with eyes closer to God's view. We are changed and no longer see ourselves or others from the centrality of our ego consciousness. In this practice of sacramental prayer, there is the possibility and hope that we may have a new depth of understanding and come to terms with our non-centrality in the cosmos. This very acknowledgment changes us and turns our prayer from one that benefits us to a prayer life of resistance.

Deepening Resistance: In-Person Communal Sacramental Prayer

My book *Embodied Liturgy* discusses the importance of embodied liturgical practices and the nature of language and rite in the creation of embodied sacramental life. The fullness of life lived in prayer and meditation is fully lived privately and with others. Nothing would make me happier than to hear, "I read your book and found an Episcopal Church." That may not be what happens. Nevertheless, I hope you will take my call to pray and to engage in a sacramental communal life with others seriously enough to find yourself a place where that can happen, if you don't already have one.

The next thing that seems very important for you, the reader, to understand is that different services within the lives of communities are meant for a variety of purposes. Let me give you an example. Those of you who are family types and have kids in tow, you may genuinely want to do what I am about to teach you to do, but you may not have the opportunity right now. That is okay; we are all of us at different points in our lives. While you may go to a family-style communal sacramental service with your kids, I encourage you to find the discipline of quiet individual prayer to buoy you up in your life. We all understand that communal prayers of one kind or another have different styles and purposes, and family services may differ from the prayer-centered communal experience you seek. That is all okay. Go where you can go; see what is out there!

I encourage you to find those deeply contemplative prayer services with the sacrament. I am in favor of congregations' having prayer spaces that are sacramental but allow for quiet. We need spaces that help provide this type of sacramental environment for those who are making a pilgrimage through their lives and seeking more profound, more meditative experiences. You can often find them early or during the week in the Episcopal Church.

What I want to do next is share with you my practice of entering communal prayer and contemplation during a sacramental service within my tradition. I attend a church with an early service when I am not working. I take my time in the morning. I usually am up and have already had some quiet time in meditation. I go and take my time, being attentive to the journey. I walk up, greet those at the church's front door, and do so quietly. I walk in, and I find a place to sit, most of the time by myself in the back. (Though sitting with people is perfectly fine too.)

A wise teacher once told me not to fidget so much. So, I have learned to calm myself and my body, as in my quiet meditation. Sometimes, I kneel during this time, and sometimes I sit. Both ways of entering the space are acceptable. The point here is to get there and be quiet. I arrive to sit and meditate in a space saturated in prayer—physically, over the years, blanketed with people's prayers and hymns.

Prayer postures are fundamental in communal prayer settings. Our bodies sharing the rhythm of the service is a good, embodied practice. Standing, kneeling, and sitting are prayer postures. Walking forward to receive communion, putting your hand out to take a piece of bread—do all this intentionally. Remember what I taught you about walking, breathing, and the importance of intentionality and attentiveness.

Consider that bowing one's head in prayer or receiving a blessing is an important prayer posture. Opening one's hands in front of you with your palms up to pray or receive a blessing is a prayer posture. It is no different than the contemplative prayer postures for the individual at home. Here, we share these in common amidst the sacramental act of the body.

When we pray, we may contemplate an image, such as an icon or cross, or focus on an object. However, I am in favor of closing our eyes. Most people do not spend much time practicing prayer, so they feel uncomfortable closing their eyes. I have learned opening your eyes, especially when you are new or not practiced, does not help; you will easily be distracted by what is going on around you. What one learns over time is that regardless of what is happening you can actually create the peaceful space by your prayer posture.

The next practice of being in God's presence during worship and prayer with others is breathing. The first time you visit will be rough, especially if you are unfamiliar with the service and how things go along. If you have never been, it will take some time to get used to it. Your prayer work is to come to a peace where your bodily presence contributes to creating the sacred space. In a small or large space, with any number of people gathered, two or three quietly holding the space of prayer will change how others enter the space. Modeling prayer in the gathering will change others' prayer practices in the same space.

At the heart of this exploration is the call to live out the Christian vision of kinship and shalom, where each act—however small—serves as a form of resistance against the dehumanizing forces of modern life as we live in our identity as the Body of Christ. Our gathered and individual prayers become a force that holds back the darkness of hopelessness and amplifies the light of divine love and peace.

Through contemplative practices, we learn to engage more deeply with our call to embody God's love in the world. Richard Rohr reminds us that prayer and action are intertwined—"two sides of the same coin" (Rohr, 2019).

Moreover, the chapter has underscored the importance of recognizing our inherent kinship with one another, a kinship not bound by race, nationality, or social status, but one rooted in our shared identity as children of God.

Our contemplation—rooted in prayer and sacrament—enables us to resist the disembodied forces of modernity, including surveillance capitalism, digital division, environmental exploitation, and the siren call of screens. Through sacramental practices, such as the Eucharist, we participate in the infinite community of God's love, drawing strength to confront these forces with courage, empathy, and a commitment to the common good (Hart, 2021; Illich, 1991). As we have seen, this resistance is not merely a reaction but a proactive stance, deeply grounded in a spiritual life that embraces both the individual and communal dimensions of faith.

It challenges us to live as communities that do not simply resist the darkness but actively spread God's light and love in the world. As we gather in prayer and break bread together, we engage in an act of justice that refocuses on God's work. We do not merely perform religious rituals—we become agents of God's shalom, co-creating a world where all creation can flourish.

Chapter Seven

Faith in Action: Ruined for Life

Resistance: Social Justice and Environmental Activism

The actual cost of discipleship is not a resigned justification of the status quo and the injustices and oppressions of an ungodly world. A discipleship rooted in a contemplative life as resistance leads to a life in the image of Jesus that is unsettling, free, and clear regarding the disparities, miseries, and divisions of a profoundly unfree world.

—A. D.

"Ruined for Life"

At a conference with my friend Tricia Lyons, one of the most engaging speakers and professors I know, Tricia shared a story that deeply resonated with me. She spoke of the Jesuit Volunteer Corps (JVC), founded in the 1950s by the Roman Catholic Jesuits in Alaska. This program invites young leaders to serve those in need, with a mission to create a more just and hopeful world by helping participants follow Jesus in grace every day.

Volunteers in the JVC are placed in impoverished urban neighborhoods and rural communities across the United States, working with homeless individuals, abused women and children, immigrants, refugees, the mentally ill, people with HIV and AIDS, and the elderly.

The JVC's goal is not only to support those in need but also to foster personal growth among the volunteers themselves. After years of this work, the young graduates of the program came up with a motto to describe their experience: "Ruined for life."

For over seventy years, the JVC program has transformed how these volunteers see, experience, and participate in the world. Wherever you find one today, they are offering their lives to Jesus Christ and trying to live differently because of their experience. Like the first disciples of Jesus, these volunteers have been "ruined for life" in the best possible way—forever changed by their encounters with Christ and the radical call to love and service.

The motto "Ruined for life" captures the essence of what it means to be a follower of Jesus in today's world: a willingness to have one's worldview upended and transformed by grace, to see the world through the lens of Christ's love and justice, and to be willing to act courageously in response to the suffering and needs of others. It reflects a deep commitment to being "ruined" in the sense of having one's previous assumptions, comforts, and securities dismantled by the reality of God's call to serve, to give, and to love without measure.

This notion of being "ruined for life" resonates particularly with our circumstances in the world today, in which there is constant connectivity, digital surveillance, economic injustice, climate crisis, and cultural tribalism, and all need faithful and radical responses. The Christian imperative to engage these problems calls on us to animate our lives in such a clear-eyed manner, vigorously enlisting the resources of our spiritual traditions, our care for justice, and our faith in God's love. If we practice unabashed faith and prayerful resistance against anti-spiritual influences, we will be ruined for life.

Our purpose will not be to escape from the world into some abstract, mystical union with God, but to dive into the world more profoundly and unashamedly as we work through prayer for justice. To dive more deeply into its pain and brokenness than we would ever risk going if we did not know that the roots of our being, the origins of everything worthy and beautiful and lasting, are powerfully held through the divine thread of love and wisdom from a loving God. We are firmly planted in our faith like an oak when we are solid and secure because of our practice. What we discover when we come to the divine in love is that our work of healing people and healing the world is to be done from a place of divine compassion rather than human reactivity. Moreover, if we find ourselves in a place of human reactivity, we must recenter ourselves and rediscover ourselves and others in relationship to the divine. Writing about the experience of contemplative prayer, Cynthia Bourgeault argues that, far from being a mystical exit point out of our suffering world, it is a form of faithful presence and hopeful engagement with suffering and injustice among our human family (Bourgeault, 2001).

We must reconsider spiritual disciplines—prayer, meditation, spiritual reflection—as a means for each of us individually and for those gathered in prayer to face the social, environmental, and economic inequalities of our world. Steeling us for truth, releasing us from denial, and calling us to account for these disciplines can give us the courage, humility, and strength we need to act with purpose in big ways and small, and help us imagine what it means to practice the presence of a life lived with Christ in such a way as others might know it.

The script of "being ruined for life" prepares the way for our discernment of how faith must now be lived and acted out as we are open to conversion: seeing the world with Christ's eyes, from the vantage point of Christ's cross, listening to the cries of the most vulnerable, and responding to the pressing demands of our own time, believing, much like those first disciples, who said: "From this moment forward, we will no longer accept anything but your words, because we have come to realize that you hold words of eternal life" (John 6:68).

Social Justice in a Digital World

Technology today both enhances and complicates the Christian vocation of witness. On the one hand, digital media can facilitate advocacy in powerful ways: information can spread quickly, movements can be exposed to greater audiences. On the other hand, digital media raises concerns about surveillance and big data, as well as adverse outcomes like community polarization.

Perhaps the most refined presentation of this framework comes from Cynthia Bourgeault. In her book, co-written, with Thomas Keeting *Centering Prayer and Inner Awakening* (2003), she suggests that contemplation is not avoidance of the world but a way of more deeply engaging with it, in keeping with an active orientation to the best kind of social justice work one can imagine. Bourgeault argues that by changing how we pay attention to everyday life, contemplative practice calls us into a mode of action that is distinguished from reactivity because it arises out of an enlarged space of awareness and discernment. Thus, the raw data of the reacting can be reconfigured into something more spacious. Here she would argue that by being attentive to removing our natural egocentrism and rejecting the dualism we seem to wrestle with constantly, we avoid being pulled in and, instead, may become compassionate to the world in any given situation.

This means that the practice of resistance becomes, through contemplation, reoriented to activism. Instead of activism that is based upon our emotions or activism based upon our family's stake in the fight, we become able to see that activism flows from a deeper place, which is in the heart of God for God's people. We seek not to locate activism and care from a newly conditioned frame of mind. Instead, it flows out of the nature of God: love, justice, and communal flourishing.

Ethical Complexity in Digital Activism

Digital activism brings unprecedented means to amplify grassroots voices and promote justice. With this comes the power of the mob. Yes, social media platforms bring a synchronicity among a diverse and expansive group. At the same time, they are not all interested in what the Christian is interested in undertaking for love's sake. A dual-minded, reflective practice for the digital age must keep all of these in focus at once. It combines prayer, practiced regularly, with sustained contemplation, and employs both as avenues for ethical discernment. The tendency with the digital will be to speed discernment up; yet taking our cue from other cultures, we understand the importance of slowing things down to do the work well.

I am now thinking of the discernment of the Ents, which are very old talking trees in the second book of *The Lord of the Rings,* entitled *The Two* Towers, by J. R. R. Tolkien (1978). In it two characters, Pippin and Merry, in a rush to save the world, meet an Ent, an ancient and wise tree named Treebeard. They ask Treebeard if the Ents can help them. He must speak with his kin first. The Ent tries to explain to them that in the old Entish language if it is worth speaking about, then it will take a long time to say and to listen. This is an example of deep prayer that brings about engagement. For such prayer to be a part of discernment, it must be practiced for a long time. After all, to sit with the divine is worth doing, for sometimes it takes a long time for the divine to speak and for us to hear.

David Bentley Hart is thoughtful regarding the interaction between Christian theology and our present context. While I was writing this book, his book *All Things Are Full of Gods* arrived (2024). In it, he continues his long exploration of computer coding as a language. He emphasizes that sober intentionality regarding technology is crucial. Pointing to the dubious desires of corporations to monetize our networked existence, he suggests that sin has, perhaps, gradually encroached upon the space we occupy.

Digital activism, like other means of interpersonal connection, can be employed for admirable or dubious, truly ethical or deceitful purposes. We cannot abdicate responsibility for its fruits and effects by insisting that sincerity is sufficient to guarantee authentic righteousness. Such a stance would be, at the very least, naïve, though never entirely without some personal merit (Hart, 2023). This is all the more reason to consider contemplation the center of all activism.

Drawing upon this wisdom, digital activism should not only be pursued as a last-ditch, moralistic act of resistance but also should flow from a genuine spiritual practice. The contemplative posture calls Christians to pause, reflect, and discern how we bring about social transformation. What I am suggesting is that more contemplation and meditation will bring about clarity, and will draw us into activism, instead of undertaking activism with some prayer attached. As Christians, we undertake activism from a deep relationship with God and other humans. Our prayer life comes not from the head but from the whole body, rooted in a relationship with different bodies and the divine.

Environmental Degradation

A global concern is shared among many humans for the health and well-being of the environment. As embodied beings, we are deeply connected to our environment and dependent upon its health and wellness. There is a saying that we must learn to repent and live lightly so all may live. Creation care is not optional for humans; it is especially not so for Christians because for Christians, God's creation is part of what we humans have an opportunity to tend. God's creation includes space, stars, planets, our galaxy, and the Earth. The great human movement of our modern era from the Industrial Revolution forward has created a very unhealthy ecosystem (water, air, resources, soil, oceans, its climate), and today we are polluting space, the moon, and other planets. We must take responsibility for the cost of destruction that we are collectively undertaking, because the cosmos is the location where our bodies dwell and in which our bodies relate to each other and the divine.

Meditation and prayer bring us into the physical awareness of many expressions of God's majesty in creation and deepen our sense of glory and wonder. When we pray with others, especially when we pray with our global neighbors in our hearts, we become mindful of the injustices of poverty and pollution that face people worldwide, particularly in the Global South and among Indigenous peoples of every land. From our prayer, we are moved with them in mind to act where we live as well as globally. The depth of our connection to the divine brings us into a life that manifests a simpler lifestyle and acts as a consumer with ecological production practices in mind. Out of the depth of prayer comes the development of awareness and words that remind us of our creation theology (Anglican Consultative Council, 2008). Prayer also brings about curiosity regarding the consumption of resources in our own lives.

Global Resource Usage by Technology and AI

The increasing speed of development and innovation concerning technology has amplified the process of human extraction of resources on a global scale. According to the 2024 UNEP (United Nations Environmental Programme) report, *Global Resources Outlook 2024*, within fifty years the volume of global resource extraction tripled, mainly driven by infrastructure expansion and the high levels of material consumption in upper-middle and high-income countries. If the current development evolution curve accelerates, then total resource extraction could grow by 60 percent by 2060 (United Nations Environmental Programme, 2024).

One of the greatest producers of rising energy use, AI requires significant amounts of electricity and cooling and, depending on the system, can have an elevated carbon footprint. Cloud data centers for AI and cloud services are already one of the fastest-growing energy consumers in the world. They account for roughly 1 percent of the world's electricity use, and as demand for AI increases, these centers are anticipated to continue using even more significant amounts of energy, according to a report that appeared in *Nature* in 2024 (Owens, 2024).

The ecological footprint of AI is not only from the energy consumption of its computation, but also the mining of new rare minerals and other raw materials for tech materials, such as hardware and batteries, which is leading to deforestation, soil erosion, and water pollution; and from the mining and processing of materials for the production and disposal of electronic devices, called e-waste. While AI can bring many benefits to various areas it is easy to ignore the fact that the efficiency of AI-driven processes exacerbates our excessive consumption of resources. Shared values between Christians and others focused on the conservation of creation and concern for the poor require scrutiny of the ecological footprint of tech cloud storage and AI technologies (Mennella et al., 2024).

Theological Responses to Environmental Challenges

From deep prayer and contemplation, humans can reconnect to their bodies and begin to understand our shared relatedness to God and other creatures. From prayer comes theology, which must craft a response to environmental despoilation by attending to the theological realities of creation care and the particular causes and practices that drive environmental degradation. Here, we understand not an exceptionalism granted to Christians by God, but a community given in creation from God. Only in this light may we face the stark realities of melting glaciers and dying coral reefs, disappearing species, and shrinking habitats. The answers will come from prayer and meditation, which leads to awareness of our problems and offers us wisdom as a path forward.

People like Bourgeault and Rohr and others invite us to a sacred activism that draws on our relationship by means of meditation and contemplation. Activism comes from prayer, deeply woven into conversation, which can be deeply revelatory when we take with us into prayer our concerns and problems. Activism at its best is engagement with the world in a deeper, more fulfilling, and more effective way—and rooted in prayer.

Expanding the Ethical Framework for Environmental Stewardship

Richard Rohr suggests that we seek our place in the whole of God's creation. We are carving out our spaces and, by our attentiveness, taking time to consider our part in the environmental collapse. We all too often look to scapegoat others. We continue our own desires and how they fit within our personal consumption. In our prayer we become free, Rohr says. We are able to be free from all else, so we can be honest and forthright with ourselves. We can, in this free space of contemplation, see differently. We can see and be in the presence of God (Rohr, 2021).

Only through deep prayer do we come to the truth of our individual responsibility and build resilience for defeating our own behaviors. Here is the prayer for the Earth held between our hands in silent contemplation that will awaken us to understand that we are the stewards of God's creation; we are called not only to conserve it, but also to heal it and refrain from harming that which God has made (Hart, 2020; Eisenstein, 2013).

Prayer Time as Activism

If you and I, along with all the other connected people, turned off and stopped using our devices for an extra three hours a day, we would actively decrease our kilowatt hour (kWh) footprint. Consider this: 923 million people live without the Internet, smartphones, and connectivity (World Data Lab, 2024). Over 80 percent of people are connected to the Internet. One person uses 187.3 kWh per year. If one person spent three or more hours disconnected and unplugged beyond what they already do, the estimated power saved per year would be 60 kWh, or a total usage of 120.07 kWh per year. If 80 percent of the global population uses 187.3 kWh, that is a total of 1.2 trillion kWh a year. If everyone decreased their usage by three hours for mediation and contemplation, the total would be 768 billion kWh. These numbers show that reducing our consumption could have significant impact.

It represents more electricity than several entire countries use in a year, could power major global cities for several years, and equates to the annual output of dozens of large power plants. Understanding these equivalents help convey just how substantial an energy savings of this magnitude truly is, with the potential to impact entire nations or multiple major cities. By disconnecting from devices and by taking seriously a technology Sabbath, we decrease the consumption of power, and with it our individual and corporate footprints.

The power of meditation is assurance and grace of God's love. For you and I will not do this work perfectly. We are going to fail despite our best efforts. We are humans who have our default settings, and we will return to our old ways. The work of regular meditation helps remind us that in failure, we may learn, and that we may always return to a God who awaits us. Here we have the image of the father's open arms when his child returns home. Here is the prodigal parent who goes against the world's ways and, though his son has wasted everything, welcomes him with open arms (Luke, 15:11–22).

Recognizing and Confronting Economic Inequality

Another theme that we face as a global community is the growing economic inequality between classes. The gap has risen in the United States in recent years for many reasons, one of which is the shifting economies from the previous era, which was still predominately a production economy, to our current one that is driven by the technological forces of a gig economy, robo-capitalism, and financial precarity that are putting our social structures under duress. I do like Shoshana Zuboff's theory of "surveillance capitalism" and how the gig economy impacts most people. The Christian response must include community support, advocacy, and ethical practices that live out Christ's justice, charity, and solidarity in and through community-based efforts, including through one's patronage of ethical businesses that put human dignity and the common good front and center.

Christians need to become more systems-sensitive about their culpability in the economic systems they want to change. In our quest for economic justice we must begin with prayer that leads to a strong enough theology that will engage our personal economies. Too often, we are all willing to protest and march without considering our own participation in the very thing causing the problem. However, because many Christians are attempting to live a type of rule of life—a regular daily practice of prayer—we must become aware and attentive to how we contribute to the problem we wish to change.

Examples include supporting living wages, advocating for fair policies, and supporting legitimate frameworks that offer economic opportunities instead of merely trying to mop up the leakages caused by inherently unequal systems. A Christian answer starts with an individual approach: responsible consumerism, ethical investment, fair employment practices, and collective advocacy for the transformation of unjust economic structures.

The Impact of the Gig Economy and Automation

Paralleling the economic divide is a growing shift toward reliance on the gig economy and automation, which not only shake up older forms of labor markets and create new forms of work, but also intensify financial insecurity for many. A common problem seen in the gig economy is that many workers end up facing precarious forms of labor with few benefits and little job security. There was resounding concern about this at the AI and Faith Ecumenical Conference in 2024.

Automation and increased efficiencies in the past have driven up productivity overall, and they also contributed to the loss of many jobs and growing income inequality. We Americans could have done better at preparing generations for the jobs needed in our job market, and we could have done better in preparing people for the gig economy that is upon us.

Christians will need to speak up for policies that serve the dignity of workers, protect workers' rights, provide just compensation, and make available reskilling and education that adjusts to new economic configurations. I agree with Richard Rohr's assessment that those who engage in contemplation will be moved to act (Rohr, 2019).

Community-Based Economic Justice Initiatives

Community-based economic justice efforts can be a vital part of how Christians address economic inequality. People who pray are moved to act. Some examples of such efforts of activism are supporting local groups that provide relational wrap-around services for those in poverty, joining living-wage campaigns and other efforts to amend market conditions to promote justice, or joining reform campaigns urging companies to become more accountable to the public. Such efforts are rooted in the conviction that economic justice is part of God's shalom in the world and that God cares greatly about the future of all creation and about the blessing of peace for all persons and communities.

Ethical Consumption and Investment

Economic injustice can also be addressed by fostering ethical consumption and investment. Christians are called to invest their time and money in businesses that value fairness, sustainability, living wages, and respect for human rights. They can purchase products they know have been produced ethically, invest their money in companies that they believe to act responsibly toward people and the environment, and take action to fight for fair trade. Applying the principle of stewardship to money is not just about how Christians can manage their finances in a God-honoring way, but also about beyond the individual, in the future, into the broader arena of economic systems, thus affecting more than just money. The call for us to act responsibly as stewards of God's creation implies changing our relationship to the whole economy. We need to commit ourselves to using our wealth in ways that further justice for the whole of creation and uphold the common good (Bourgeault, 2003).

The Role of the Church in Promoting Economic Justice

The Church must be a voice for economic justice that calls out the sin of inequality. Christians must know how they can take on personal responsibility for economic action by organizing communities around the empirical study of how and why we are failing to bring about justice and peace. Faith communities can be the drivers of transformational change through community organizing, social education, and advocacy, bringing together the many actors in the economy to advocate for livable change. They can stand as pastoral beacons for the poor by creating food banks, encouraging financial literacy, offering employment resources, and other direct, stabilizing interventions while, at the same time, circulating models of generosity and solidarity that emulate the Kingdom of God.

Integrating Contemplative Practices with Economic Advocacy

Spiritual practices, such as prayer, meditation, and contemplation, create a reflective space that grounds economic justice work in the spiritual life. Cynthia Bourgeault reminds me always that we are not trying to escape the world. We are instead becoming strengthened for our presence in the world (Bourgeault, 2003). We seek a depth of attentiveness to the divine and others so that we may be in the world and share in our responsibility of bodily presence. By grounding advocacy in spiritual experiences, the individual thus grounds their life in an awareness of divine and human bounty. Everyone who deeply meditates understands that they have something (whether it be a little or a lot) to offer. We are given a bounty in our very being. Our prayer enlightens our hearts for the doing of good work in God's name and the sharing of gifts and monies to help deal with impoverishment of every kind in human society. Our economic justice work is marked by purpose, clarity, and compassion—and by holding these in tension, our work remains aligned with a Christlike spirit. In this way, Christians can seek to mirror the love, justice, and mercy experienced in prayer from God to a world suffering from poverty and inequality.

Division, Racism, and Cultural Tribalism in a Digital Age

We have unfortunately brought with us into the age of the Internet of Things (IoT) our divisions. In fact, social media has helped us to amplify unhealthy voices of division, racism, and cultural tribalism. Digital stereotypes and hate speech have soared, underpinned by algorithmic support. X (formerly Twitter) is a good example of concerns about algorithmic control by a few tech oligarchs. Moreover, users are multiplying visitations to sites that are racist, white supremacist, xenophobic, and disseminating untrue and contentious content

(Anti-Defamation League, 2024). Algorithms tend to boost posts with each interaction, irrespective of whether that is 100 likes or 100 dislikes, or insults, or racist slurs. In other words, there is no truly moderating effect by these algorithms.

Christians and Christian communities have been at a loss to combat these forces. As an example, even though the Institute for the Future (IFTF.com) did a custom report for the Episcopal Church in 2008 that showed this was going to happen and that the Church had an opportunity to imagine how to strengthen its own witness, very little was done. In part, this was due to organizational shortsightedness when it comes to the future of technological trends. Christians have the opportunity to contest these forces actively by fostering peacebuilding, empathic understanding, and reconciliation online and in person. Moreover, Christian communities themselves are so divided and have not been able to be either unified in their own stance or unified as a community (Subsplash and Barna, 2022).

Surveillance Capitalism and Its Role in Division

As Shoshana Zuboff has pointed out in her book *Surveillance Capitalism*, we are undergoing a massive expansion of previously unthinkable forms of commodification. Our personal data and digital footprint offer predictive behavior to the owners of the platforms, and automated personalization adds immense power to the processes that transform human behavior under conditions not chosen or controlled by the individual (Zuboff, 2020).

When people are isolated, race and culture can deepen into chasms of misinterpretations as they emerge through media. Information poverty (people with less technology and connectivity) deepens trenches while more extreme news sources create ghettoes of mis- and dis-information. We believe our tribe is right.

Our isolation behind digital walls amplifies these poor relationships; the endless layering of insulation from our personal information and the structural insulation of our social institutions ensures that rather than seeking the stimulus and creativity brought about by difference, we avoid it. Interestingly, we know that the human brain considers the future like it considers strangers (Zimbardo & Boyd, 2010; Ersner-Hershfield et al., 2008). We do not naturally react well to those who are different or bring different ideas, and we do not naturally react well when we consider our future. What that suggests is that we as a species have a hard time imagining the future anyway, but this is made more difficult by our tribal differences.

People, families, groups, and nations are imprisoned in informational silos made by self-referencing pseudo-facts: it becomes possible to sleepwalk into tyranny and genocide by denying the truth of evidentiary reality—let alone God—made human dignity. Again, I believe that prayer through conversation with the divine and sitting quietly and being more connected with the people in our lives and communities brings about resistance to human tribalistic tendencies.

Resistance Recap: Awareness, Resistance, and Advocacy

A Christian response to the crisis we face globally under the weight of technology and constant connectivity will evolve and involve practices of discernment, pushback, and advocacy. At stake is digital justice, for both the data producer and the data consumer, and a defense of the sacredness of personal data and dignity. For Christians, this will involve advocating for rights to transparent data practices and data regulation in the name of human dignity. In addition to this, it will call for support of policies that enforce a data privacy right and that regulate the collection and use of data such that it does not violate personal protections.

Meditation helps us to see each other with the eyes of Christ from his vantage point upon the cross. Our prayer time with the divine will quietly and pervasively eat away at our projections of imperfection placed upon others by helping us realize that we too are imperfect. Unless we are narcissists (and some of us are), we can realize that our human formation has brought us to doubt and shame; our "Godly gaze" helps us to rethink our very being. Our creation, preservation, and the very gift of life given by God have granted us dignity. We, in all our bodily shapes, colors, sizes, and visible and invisible differences, are beautiful in the eyes of God, and so we may become beautiful in each other's eyes. Yet, I hasten to say that it is not our eyes that grant dignity, but rather God's vision and creation. It is seeing through the eyes of God, and it is God's gaze, that truly grants dignity. What we do is to act through God's vision of each other.

In meditation, we are granted the ability to see from a different perspective—God's loving gaze. With the eyes of Christ, we are given empathy for dismantling hate and division that shape tribalism. This will always come out of embodied togetherness. Contemplating the greatness of God's diverse creation, by meditating and praying in groups, and working across tribal boundaries of every kind, will bring us to a new age of human culture where we can say with a resounding clarity from every religion in the world, and Christianity especially, that there is no race or creed (Galatians 3:28). Let us see as God sees.

Additionally, as embodied creatures intentional about shaping contemplative practices, we can learn through prayer and meditation the practice of an inner posture of silence and discernment, such that we gain by perceiving in a way that is closer to God's way of perception. We begin to see the relationship between all things and all humans and that nothing is ever alone or separate from multitudinal relationships. This attunement to our place, and the place of all things, in eternal connectivity to the cosmos allows us to reject both a purely scientific understanding that reality is out there or a purely philosophical understanding that we make reality through our consciousness. Our attentiveness assists us in an experience of interwovenness with God and cosmos.

This contemplative attentiveness offers a platform from which Christians can approach one another in life. I wonder what might happen if Christian leaders, Jewish leaders, Muslim leaders, and a host of other non-Abrahamic faiths got together to sit quietly and listen to words from God. What might we hear together? How long might we sit together—for days, months, or years? What if Christians themselves did this? Imagine that. We all want to talk; yet for us to come together, we might need to sit together without words for a while, in the in-betweenness amidst God and each other. This is one way we can, together, offer a sign of resistance to the world order. Where everything is urgent, there is not time to sit down for prayer to the same God, and so on and on we go, spending so many words without ever finding peace.

Resistance Against Gender Violence, Global Conflict, Religious Freedom, and Food Insecurity

Within my tradition, there is a shared global concern regarding each of these topics. Gender-based violence, global conflict and nation state violence, a lack of religious freedom and the rise of theocracies, and food insecurity are sins deeply rooted in our human mimetic desire and sibling rivalry. Each of these deserves its own weighty discussion—and in my tradition we are doing that and having global conversations on interventions. We are building partnerships and eroding the powers that drive this horrific human-on-human violence and inequality.

Why are these discussions important? Humans were and are made in the image of God (Genesis 1:26–28), and each person has inherent dignity. In Christ, humanity is offered new birth into a living hope (1 Peter 1:3) and is called to love God and its neighbor (1 John 4:11). To be at peace and care for one's neighbor is an ancient belief in many religions, yet it seems to be the hardest for us to understand. I believe that is because to love your "neighbor" does not in our culture mean to love everyone. However, Jesus calls us to love our neighbor and shows in the parable about the Samaritan that the neighbor is completely different than we are. So, the fact that we define *neighbor* as something within our comfort zone, or a noun with no responsibility attached, is a radical departure from the Bible's passages, which speak of mutual care of one another by virtue of our sacred text and Jesus's teaching—not by virtue of our personal relationship with another person. This is also a departure from basic humanism. The idea of a detached neighbor with no responsibility fits well within a self- and ego-buffered society that views everything with a self-centered awareness of relationships.

The diversity of humanity, present from the Garden's first male and female, is an unmitigated good. At Pentecost, the people of God were filled with the plurality of cosmic tongues because they were to go out and bless and multiply God's peace—shalom. The fullness of this vision in Revelation 7:9 has no concept of an ethnically homogeneous Heaven. And so, even though humanity is estranged by our relational brokenness, in Christ, the image of God still shines forth from every person and through all bodies. The goodness of life can be spoiled because of the apparent abundance of human corruption. All life is considered sacred within the Church; all persons possess inherent dignity. It is the position of the Church that all persons deserve to have the conditions of life that will allow them to experience the fullness of life. Therefore, for example, any gender-based violence works against God's good news of open arms and love.

Again, the image of the prodigal father comes to us. This father and son story is an image of God and God's love. It is a prodigal, extravagant love that does not work like the world, and instead offers love irrespective of return. I believe that divine connection and a permeable interior life, where love flows in from the divine and love flows out into the lives of others, built over years of prayer, show God's extravagant love. We too are invited to be like divine love and give without care of the return on our investment. If you love those who love you, what credit to you is that? The reward is in the prodigal nature of love that is like God's (Luke 6:32). In prayer and contemplation, we come to understand that Jesus loved his own friends until the very end, but they were not the only ones that he loved (John 13:1).

Anglican and Episcopal people are raising their voices in concern over global conflict and are coming together to encourage peacebuilding. We share this with all the religions of the world—that we may live in harmony and peace. Here, Christians call this the work of reconciliation and peacebuilding among all humans. Yes, conflicts among nations have been with us a long time. Current global crises have created millions of refugees and internally displaced persons who are impoverished and struggling for daily survival. Combined with climate-crisis-caused migration and violence in Central and South America, we are experiencing the largest migratory mass movement in human history.

Currently, churches are reaching out, resettling refugees, offering support to politicians for peace actions, building alliances, lobbying for policy change, and cultivating care for the environment in every setting, and at every level. Funds are raised for food, water, chaplains, refugee resettlement, and economic opportunities so refugees may find funds to make their journey. Rebecca Stevens, founder of Thistle Farms, and her work with the Syrian refugees and those in Central and South America, is an example of one person's action that comes from deep prayer and contemplation.

We cannot find peace without prayer and contemplation. As Mother Theresa of Calcutta said, "The fruit of silence is prayer, the fruit of prayer is faith, the fruit of faith is love, the fruit of love is service, and the fruit of service is peace" (Vardey & Theresa, 1995, 16). Often, followers of Jesus go immediately to service and do not stop to begin with prayer. We need prayers of discernment, prayers for wisdom, prayers for finding our own peace amid the world around us. We often look around our neighborhoods, towns, cities, states, at a national or global level and feel anxiety or even fear. Then we rush to action. Yet for those of us who have walked a pilgrim path with others who have experienced the world over decades, we set out daily upon a long journey until our day ends and our hearts rest in God.

There is so much pain and suffering in the world—something many great wisdom teachers have seen and experienced over centuries. So many then have said to their followers, as Jesus said to those who followed him, come away with me and let us pray. Prayer brings peace and peaceful action. The longer it is practiced, the deeper one goes, the more one may discover a great peace beyond understanding such that we are not blown around by the winds of change, war, and political instability (Philippians 5:7). We need people who are peace bringers, peace givers, and peacemakers, for they are blessings to us in our times of need. In peace, we are known as children of God (Matthew 5:9).

Food and water security are also of concern for many around the globe because of shortages created by climate change. There is a global need for activism linked to weather change, failed crops, war, economic imbalances among countries, and class disparities within cultures.

The nature of quiet and listening is key to discernment before action and activism. A post in 2011 by Brian McLaren affected me and how I think about grace and prayer that interrupt our lives by resisting the urge for impersonalized eating, shopping, and preparing food. The fact that this came during a time of my own discernment with a monk friend amplified my thoughts on the matter. In prayer, we are reminded that the very creation of the world is a garden. We must breathe and stop and consider the colors of the food we eat and how diverse they are; after all, how many shades of green are there (McLaren, 2011)? We should also consider how our food feels in our hands. I am reminded here of the book *The Supper of the Lamb*, by Robert Farrar Capon (1969). In it he begins with this note:

> Next take one of the onions (preferably the best-looking), a paring knife, and a cutting board and sit down at the kitchen table. Do not attempt to stand at a counter through these opening measures. In fact, to do it justice, you should arrange to have sixty minutes or so free for this part of the exercise. Admittedly, spending an hour in the society of an onion may be something you have never done before. (Capon, 1969, 17)

In these few words, just as McLaren invited, we are reminded that we are in relationship with God's creation. So, we give thanks for warm sun, rain, soil, air, seed, seasons that bring to us the fruit provided. We are in awe that we get to have this for ourselves. How can we not give thanks to God, weather, and the hands that toiled and tilled the land for our food?

Perhaps then we might be led to consider the people who brought this to us. Consider the people, the men and women who come to work in our stores every day and stock shelves and wax floors and work the cash registers and pack the groceries. How good it is that they are there to help us to have food to eat! Think of the drivers and sailors who bring us our food from the farm or around the world to the store. This then puts us in the mind of those who plant, grow, and work in the sun to bring us such food, often making 50 cents per 32-pound (bucket full in the case of tomatoes in Immokalee, Florida [McLaren, 2011]). So, we appreciate as we ponder farmwork and pray for just and living wages for all people who labor. Perhaps this brings us to even understand our scripture and the pastoral parables of farm and vineyard workers.

Being thankful in the presence of God in our silent time and at our tables leads to gratitude spoken at the store, or to a farmer, or to a worker. It recalls our part of the work of fairness too. Tables of plenty and prayer remind us of those who go without. All of this helps us to become mindful of the opportunity that we can be involved in just practices when it comes to food production; and to be attentive to and aware of our links to people in this chain of production. To work for the farmer, the baker, the migrant workers, the sower of seeds, and those who need food, water, and resources is an act of gratitude that brings resistance.

The Industrial Revolution and now the Internet of Things have quieted our realization that we are bodies dependent upon other bodies and the earth for our very existence. Moreover, we are mostly ignorant of how our choices cause global shifts. In our deep prayer we can hear the voices of our global kin and the sounds of creation (including the nonhuman voices) who are hungry and thirsty. We can have visions of our future on this planet and dream the dream of healing that which is so very broken. We have learned in these years that fungi and trees and animals all have forms of being with each other and work together. We are unable to see such things, so we must spend time listening.

Attentiveness in prayer to water and food is resistance to mindlessness and the false idea that we provide for ourselves when we actually rely on whole communities of people and God for what we receive. In prayer there is also the resistance to consumption. In my tradition, and others, we call this fasting. For those of you who observe fasting as part of a season, the fasting I am talking about is much more than not eating certain foods or taking up a new activity or ministry while fasting from another. Fasting is an ancient prayer discipline that is present in each of the Abrahamic faiths and is revealed in our shared scripture.

We have talked about Sabbath from electronic devices, and this certainly applies here. But let us talk about fasting as a contemplative action. Fasting is an ancient spiritual practice in which a person abstains from food or drink for an extended period to focus the attention of the spirit and the senses on the will of God. Such discipline, carried on through the history of the Hebrew prophets of the Old Testament, the early Christian communities, and into the practices of millions of religious people today, is motivated by the desire to reject the demands of the body to seek nourishment for the soul. Fasting, by definition, denies the appetites and distractions of bodily existence to provide a time and place in which to become more aware of the presence of God, the nature and extent of personal and communal sin, and the need for repentance, and a spiritual redirection of life. Fasting is an act of humility, penitence, and devotion, one in which the mind and heart become attuned to the divinity of a loving God, rather than lost in the confusion of self-interest.

From the beginning, fasting was linked to the Sabbath as a complementary, intentionally disruptive practice meant to lead the faithful into progressively deeper communion with God. Sabbath is the weekly pause for worship and meditation—ceasing from labor so that creation and liberation might be honored. This is disruptive to the rhythms of daily life. Together, fasting and the Sabbath usher the faithful into a ritual of rhythmic praxis, where the cycle of devotion directs us toward a place of awareness and attention. Sabbath is by its very nature an act of resistance to the frenetic nature of a life of consumption.

Fasting from food and water can be a powerful protest—against systemic voraciousness, injustice, and oppression. Fasting against a greedy consumerist culture is an exercise in voluntary nonconsumption, criticizing a culture choking on consumption. Fasting against the present life of constant connectivity and consumerism puts us in touch with how our own spirit hungers for respite. In struggles for social or political change, fasting can become a nonviolent protest, or what might be called a practice that expresses solidarity with the oppressed and their injustice, and an act of drawing attention to their plight. It is a dissonant embodied protest. It is an extended embodied prayer (meaning it is more than silence or words) that challenges comfort, includes moral reflection, and aligns the fasting individual with the suffering others. This amounts to saying, "This is not as God wills" to systemic inequality and suffering.

When we agree to the invitation to be ruined for life, we enter another kind of reorientation—one that shatters our illusions about safety, calls into question our deepest assumptions about privilege, comfort, and righteousness, and asks us to dive into a life of courage and compassion and justice. We are called, as Christians, to be among and of the world—but not to be in it by virtue of our human reactivity. Depth of understanding and activism rooted in mindfulness and contemplation is not an act of the world. By the tools of compassion that are the product of a robust spiritual discipline, we deeply connect to the wellspring that some call the heart of Christ. Such a holistic reorientation allows spiritual disciplines—prayer, contemplation, and meditation—to change our view of the world, to enable us to become conscious of how prayer is ultimately a resistant act that interrupts life as usual.

It is in a world of bodies numbed by screens, beset by economic poverty, environmental degradation, and cultural fracture, that the Christian vocation becomes so radically countercultural. In a world hungry for authentic hope, to be "ruined for life" is to commit to radical discipleship—to live as witnesses of Christ's love. It is to challenge ourselves to see things the way that Christ sees, to hear the things that Christ hears, and to speak the things that Christ speaks, to bear the things that Christ bears, and to fight the battles that Christ fights. This is our invitation, challenge, and hope: to allow ourselves to be changed by grace so thoroughly that we can no longer see the world or our place within it the same way. This vocation begins with prayer.

Chapter Eight

Unabashed Faith—Living an Authentic, Resilient, Christian Life

Resistance: Create a Rule of Life

An unabashed faith dares to hope so fiercely that it becomes a quiet rebellion against a world whispering falsehoods of spiritual disembodiment that claims connection while delivering loneliness.
— A. D.

An unabashed faith is not about believing. Unabashed faith is about having a hope so powerful that its way of life is itself a resistance to the forces of anti-embodied spirituality, constantly whispering to every part of our lives that it is real, when it is not. In this final chapter, I wish to put together the thoughts of the previous chapters under the heading of a life lived in faith day to day in a world that too often seems to be stacked against the most deeply held spiritual and communal practices. At a time of great technological innovation, a new digital economy that creates uncertainty, a global techno-oligarchy, and ever-increasing consumerist momentum, we ask: how might we sustain a living, breathing Christian ethos?

In trying to answer this question, we must recognize some of the internal tensions of contemporary life. We live amid unparalleled interconnection. With a simple click of a finger, we can reach out across a continent and blast our messages to individuals near and far. But paradoxically, it is also an era in which many people sense that they are more alone and more fragmented than ever before; where it never seems possible to find silence; and where nearly all our day is increasingly mediated by screens. It is an era where it seems that all the world has to offer is at our fingertips, and yet where we are often aching for something more—something deeper, and more abiding, more authentic than what consumer culture has bequeathed to us. Therefore, this chapter intends to be a sort of map—a way to engage with these complexities that starts with the practices and resources of an unapologetic Christianity and helps to hold us steady as we navigate.

There's nothing intrinsically good or bad about technology: it's our use of it that matters. The omnipresent smartphone, for instance, while a fabulous testament to human ingenuity, is also a distraction from stillness. Social media is an online space that enables us to share community and support each other. Still, it's also a massive dumping ground for viciousness, hatred, racism, white supremacy, posturing, pettiness, voyeurism, and distortion of self-identity, valorization, and subjugation. At its worse it is all these things and more.

There are ways that technology can be used to support each other, our mutual pilgrimages, and spiritual growth. To this commitment we must apply a fruitful practice of intentionality, boundary-setting, fasting, and Sabbaths. We must learn for the sake of our bodies to restrict the amount of time spent with the machine(s) so that we make possible the space needed to engage contemplatively with the world.

May I suggest that you inventory your use of technology? Assessment questions that could be helpful include: How much time are you spending online? What are your primary/regular uses of digital tools, channels, and platforms? What do you think/feel when you are spending time online? Surfing the web? On Facebook? YouTube? On other social media outlets? Are there patterns that seem to be spiraling you away from your spiritual goals in some way?

Embracing Digital Spaces for Faith

Social media, the Internet, and digital spaces provide unprecedented opportunities for evangelical outreach and provisional communion. Churches can air services; hold virtual Bible studies; prayer groups; give space to individuals to share their journeys; share prayers via blogs, podcasts, and social media; and connect people who have never met face to face. These are new ways people are already connecting for the sake of the Gospel, especially among those isolated or unable to gather with fellow sojourners.

As we seize on these opportunities, we must remember to stay connected to the flesh and blood that grounds our faith to the earth and to Christ. We are embodied creatures. The private life of prayer and silence, the shared sacraments, the liturgy, and in-person fellowship—these are important aspects of the Christian life. For those who cannot come to be with others in community I suggest that community must be attentive enough to go to them. Expressions of faith online must augment these practices but not replace them. They must lead us deeper into the mystery of God's truth and help us live out our faith incarnationally.

Resistance Recap: Developing a Rule of Life

Another way forward is for you to develop a "rule of life." A rule of life is a pattern and a rhythm of practices that can enable us to live out the call of our faith each day. My rule of life is connected to a monastic community in Boston called the Society of Saint John the Evangelist, and I practice it regularly and have done so for twenty years. It includes the following: time for prayer daily, marking days of fasting on Fridays and in preparation for holy days, and taking a weekly Sabbath. I also have a confessor that I go to, and I commit to one week-long retreat a year. The last thing in my rule is a commitment to support in prayer and with funds the society itself, which I do. You can develop your rule of life with the help of a priest, spiritual director, or a monk or nun who is available in your area, and willing to do so. I have included the information on the rules of the society I am in a relationship with in the bibliography. You might visit various websites and seek out an Episcopal or other group that can help. Simply type into your search engine "rule of life" and see what comes up.

A rule of life comes out of prayer. It is tough to create the rule without prayer and discernment. Draft the rule and begin to use it and pray about it. The rule of life must be held in prayer and quiet as you ponder your commitment to it. You must also be flexible enough for the rule to evolve as needed. For instance, my rule of life did not include digital Sabbaths until this summer.

I used to practice it intentionally; however, during COVID constant connectivity became solidified in my daily waking hours. So, I begin again.

I am inviting you to join me and make sure you take a digital Sabbath or fasting as you begin to draft your rule of life. This rule might be a set of boundaries or guidelines that reinforce the life-giving dimension of one's day (for example, a ritual of thirty minutes of prayer and reading scripture daily when your phone is unplugged, or simply less time on social media). This might be detailed as ways of fasting or Sabbath. Get your phone to help you manage your day along with your outlook. Make the machine work for your spiritual life and not the other way around.

If we commit to a rule of life that repositions the traditional collection of spiritual disciplines into the regularity of life, we will see increased health and vitality (Psalm 25). In this way, media consumption becomes an adjunct to our daily life. An unabashed faith believes that life with God is essential, and it further believes a life lived in love of neighbors is a life worth living. If that is true, we must beg the question: What honest amount of life are you giving to God and for the good of neighbors each day?

Looking Forward: The Future of Faith in a Digital World

Our capacity to navigate the future of faith, and have faith in the future, is our potential. I firmly believe this is so. However, it will only work if faith through embodied prayer, embodied community, and embodied action balances the Internet of Things and emerging AI evolution. Through practice, we have more profound days of meaning (1 Peter 2:2).

By what we say and what we do, by what we trust and what we reject, by what we hope for and what we fear, by what we do and do not do, by whose voice we choose to amplify, and by which we choose to silence, we can remove our now digitally immersed and directed lives into new and living water, anchoring in deep, mindful dependence on God and one another in the midst of God's creation (Matthew 4:4).

The Role of Community and Spiritual Practices

Embodied community in real life has always been and will always be the outward expression of community and spirituality that, against the backdrop of growing rampant individualism, selfishness, and personal ambition, lies at the core of Christian faith. The Church can provide a radical rebuttal of the solipsistic indulgence of our current (mostly disembodied) social networks. This community life is revealed and formed by the love of Christ, and whose practices of prayer, meditation, worship, remembrance, and proclamation are all undertaken communally. We must become a different kind of people who are connected to the divine, and who worship God not only with our lips but with our lives (Matthew 15:8).

Community as a Sacred Space for Growth and Transformation

Christian faith is "ecclesial"; this is to say, it is created, summoned, and held together by and in its communal gathering. It is in the community that we find a place of holiness, home, care, common good, and mutual transformation. It is in the community that we learn to love the neighbor, that we receive the promise of forgiveness, and that we, in turn, become the community of forgiveness, graced by God, and gracing each other within and without our community.

The fullest embodiment of our faith takes place in organized communal worship and the routines of the liturgy. Gathering with other Christians for worship, prayer, and the sacraments is a crucial activity as a member of Christ's body. In such communal worship, we encounter God differently through the senses. We also become aware that we are joined in our seeking.

Community is where we find a countercultural antidote to the shallowness and alienation of digital life. Face-to-face communion draws us closer. Sabbaths of prayer together enable us to see the face of Christ in others, where our ears can be attentive, and where brothers and sisters weep, mourn, and rejoice as one. People are feeling the cultural vacuum of relational and spiritual impoverishment. The Church can be the place for those need who need healing (Galatians 6:1–2).

Spiritual Practices: The Foundation of Resilient Faith

Spiritual disciplines, prayer and meditation, even lament and communal lament (which many reading this may have experience in), and contemplation and fasting orient us anew under the umbrella of God's grace. Embodied spiritual practices are how we recover and recalibrate, return to God's purposes. They are not magic or arbitrary rituals—we are transformed, co-formed, and renewed into the image of Jesus as the Spirit moves through us outwardly into the world.

The Interplay of Community and Practice

Individual and corporate prayer are two sides of the same coin. When we take our private prayer life into the community and share prayer, a hymn, or scripture, we create memory paths of embodied practices. We find that the two practices build upon one another. Just as a meditation and prayer life will make the gathering itself deeper, so too will a word spoken in a gathering enter our contemplative prayer life for a sitting or a week of sittings.

We are aware of one another and our surroundings in a complex way. We are interconnected by the sound of our voices and how our prayer intercessions mix, how our bodies sit together within a space, and so much more. The community that prays together and thus ministers together and worships together lives a particular reality of Christ's compassion and love. It is unique every time we gather and wholly different than prayer alone. This is the visible witness of the kingdom of God (Hebrews 10:24–25). Only when we gather do we have these types of experiences.

Resisting Dehumanization and Consumerism

In this day and age, when, in many ways, life seems more technologized and consumerized, there is much to be said for resisting the kind of world that shrinks you to being nothing but an ever-hungry consumer. Belonging to a group that is countercultural is an embodied, empowering act.

The dangers of dehumanizing consumerization are legion. What does it mean to dehumanize? It means we no longer see ourselves and others as fully and authentically human. Dehumanization means that we treat ourselves and others as though we, or they, are things, objects, as statistics, as resources, or, at worst, mere means for some other end. All of us can do this in ways that are subtle and complex. Algorithmic attention groups us by our interests, thereby removing diverse conversations and creating more surface-assured assumptions about each other.

The problem this creates is that while we wish for human dignity and flourishing, we are herded by technology into like-minded groups. We become a new kind of chattel for economic and technological dependence. We are individuals who are transactionally summated as disparate data points for advertisers. We are manipulated (according to the logic of the platform-owners' preferences) in order to generate revenue for owners.

We are being determined and divided against one another by platforms that are manipulated, turning our bodies and emotions into bondage. This is dehumanizing our bodies. We can compare this to indentured servitude. What has been offered to us as free use is a process whereby we become dependent upon our technology and social media while our emotions, creativity, personal data, and experiences are being scraped and turned into profits by shareholders, companies, and private owners.

Consumerism encourages us to cultivate value conventions that designate our own worth in relation to the things that we own and purchase; we do this again when we try to bring our half-formed identity to full fruition by finishing who we are with the new device we got, the fashion we bought, or what we managed to capture and present of ourselves to others via social media. This kind of dehumanizing poses the threat of a utilitarian ethic of profit, gain, and efficiency in place of people, and compassion consumption in place of concern. We become less than fully human—less enfleshed, less loving, less creative, less fully participative, less accountable to each other, less connected by a sense of interrelatedness, and less open to creation and God.

Embracing a Life of Purpose and Simplicity

Resisting those forces begins with choosing to live another way, a choice of faith that resists the story that we are consumers in a market, and we must participate in enrolling others. It is a commitment to remain in fidelity to a life of intimacy and simplicity defined by who we are—beloved daughters and sons of God.

Simple living, then, is not a practice of poverty and renunciation, but of reduction in handing over space for disordered distraction. In simple living we rediscover what is essential. This book has been about the need for examination and then reduction of our addictions to technological devices, and a reduction of addiction to possessions, or perhaps in the experience of things. Simple living through a prayerful and attuned life is then one of deeper connectedness with the world and cosmos which is active. It is a rejection of the Newtonian view of a universe of items and instead an engagement with an animated world of relationships. It is also a resistance against the commodification of one another through technology and the commodification of God's cosmos and world. Simple living is the outward sign of a life of interdependence where we recognize our being a part of the creation and not independent from it.

Jesus said, "For what shall it profit a person if he shall gain the whole world, and lose his own soul?" (Mark 8:36). Each of us arrives after a lived life with encumbered likes and dislikes, judgments, convictions, headaches, wounds, and joys. The practice of a life lived with God creates the strength of an inner life that helps us discover the purpose of life is to live for God and to live for others and for the creation. This is an unabashed faith; this is resistance.

Ethical Engagement: A Call to Action

In other words, to refuse to be dehumanized is to act ethically in a society that is captive to a human-created tool that intends to remake the world and disembody it. It is to fight against systems and structures of exploitation and oppression. It is to clamor for justice and to stand with the dehumanized and oppressed. Ethical living can mean choosing what and where we buy to buy things, and where we invest. It can mean deciding to try to be greener in our practices. Ultimately, it means speaking out and using our voices and social capital to assist others in discovering a more dignified way of living and relating. This is the way we create a society that seeks the flourishing of all people. Ethical engagement is resistance by living out your faith in committed, concrete ways. This means seeing the image of God in everyone and then acting in such a way as to protect that image.

Finding Strength in Faith to Resist

Resistance to dehumanization and rampant consumerism takes work. It is costly. Such a life entails commitment and a routine of practice. However, we do not do it in a vacuum: we do it in the power of a lived prayer life, and a prayer life rooted in communities that give us insight. By building on these insights our resistance is grounded in a shared hope that echoes what is revealed by scripture. This tradition informs the Church and invites us to a pattern based on the life of Christ himself, who suffered and died resisting the exclusionary, unjust, and oppressive forces of our collective individualism. This resistance flows from unabashed faith, which sustains us as we stand together amid a dominant culture that defaces that faith; a culture that habituates us to a life of sacred obedience to lesser gods.

An unabashed faith flows from a full of life of prayer, abundant life of gratitude, whole life of flourishing, a life lived in rich kinship relations directed toward God and neighbor. I promise you that when life is done, it will be a life embraced by the love of God, lived for others, and a life shared with friends and family that matters most.

Embracing an Unabashed Faith Is a Commitment to Resist

I have offered that a life of prayer is an act of thoughtfulness in the face of dehumanization and consumerism. It liberates us, frees us to live mindfully, and to live for meaning toward God's Kingdom instead of the marketplace, so that we can see each other, all of us, as children of God, not consumers, not statistics, not click-throughs.

We must integrate technological life by approaching it with a proper perspective, anchoring our existence in both community and spiritual practices, and resisting the dehumanizing pressures of an often disembodied lifestyle. In so doing, we learn to say no to capitalism's siren call and find a more straightforward, modest, better-connected way to live. We recover and embrace a more embodied worship, a more prosperous, more vibrant communal existence, through which we can embrace the reality of divinity not by ourselves, but together.

This has not merely been a theoretical discussion—it is a call to life. The concrete, active steps elaborated here are not mere prescriptions—they are pathways into a theophanic way of life—a life lived in faith open to a radically simple possibility of God-with-us.

Ultimately, living an unabashed faith means more than believing—it means living out that belief in every facet of life, resisting anti-spiritual influences. It means being fully present, fully human, and fully alive to the divine spark in your life so as to discover that you are a miracle.

Acknowledgments

As you well know, a book is never the product of one individual. I am grateful for JoAnne Doyle, who is always my first reader, with a critical eye and red pen in hand. I wish to say, too, that Fiona Hallowell has been an amazing partner and editor in this project. This was a difficult book to produce for a variety of reasons. I am indebted to both JoAnne and Fiona for believing in the project. They both buoyed me up when I flagged. Their support and encouragement brought this to fruition. Fiona's editing helped to make this an excellent readable text with a flow—I am so thankful.

I am grateful for Dr. Ben Fulford and Dr. Wayne Morris, who reminded me that writing "is a bishop's work." I am called to teach and to be an apologist for Christ and God's mission. Those words capture their support perhaps in a bit more flowery "Andy Doyle" way; nevertheless, these words came just at the right time, as I was so frustrated with the writing. They did not even know what a gift they were. Thank you.

A bishop's schedule is forever a jumbled mess. There is never any time for another thing, and I tend to commit and squeeze several different work weeks, multiple projects, and meetings into one week. There is no possible way that I could have the time to write without my team. In particular here I wish to mention The Rev. Canon Christine Faulstich, The Rev. Canon Marcea Paul, Sara Marlatt, and Julie Paré. They help protect my creative time while getting me everywhere I committed to go and seeing everyone I committed to seeing. They are my time-turners, and I am so fortunate to get to work with them.

This book was deeply influenced by a continuing conversation in my head with David Bentley Hart, David Chalmers, Iain McGilchrist, Shoshana Zuboff, Katherine Pickstock, and Jonathan Haidt. The mind, the body, consciousness, the soul, technology, and technological capitalism are conversations that the theologian needs to be a part of as apologist, prophet, pastor, and teacher.

Appendix
Questions of the Novice

Here are a few questions that typically arise as you begin a practice of prayer, as a beginner or as someone returning to contemplative prayer:

Is contemplative prayer biblical?

Contemplative prayer is rooted in the scriptures. Numerous passages speak about coming in silence and in quietness to seek the face of God: "Be still and know that I am God . . ." (Psalm 46:10). Jesus himself, for example, often took time away in solitary places to pray. This can teach us to pray with God, to be quiet in the presence of God, to listen for His voice, and to be formed more into his image.

What does it mean to "be present"?

When people say, "Be present," it is simply about bringing your full attention to this moment—noticing what is around you and what is happening inside you, without judgment. It is about gently returning your attention to where your body is, here and now, rather than to some imagined state of being or being without intention or attention.

Will I be able to quiet my mind completely?

You are not meant to quiet the mind completely (if your mind chatter is robust, there is nothing to be ashamed of), and it is natural for the mind to be active during sitting meditation. The point is to become aware of thoughts without being taken over by them—like a person can watch a river flow without jumping in.

Is it okay if I get distracted?

Yes, even a practiced contemplative gets distracted. Are we all troubled by distractions while we meditate? Distractions can be children, parents, siblings, laughter, a chiming clock, a delivery of mail, your cat has the zoomies, all while your thoughts jump from planning a birthday to an article on devastating world news. Your contemplative work is to notice, and each time your mind wanders, gently bring it back to your chosen point of attention—return, return, return.

What if I do not feel anything special?

It does not matter if you feel anything in particular; this is not only common but a good sign. Your meditation does not have to be about anything, and at the same time, it can be about everything that arises. It is best to see the value in your meditation as being not in any single moment but in your whole meditation practice. The rewards of meditation are more likely to show themselves over time and emerge gradually and subtly; do not expect dramatic effects. The body and how it experiences this work is not one of certainty but of possibility.

How do I know if I am doing it right?

There is no right. The world and our bodies so influence us as human beings that cleansing our minds and spirits to connect to the divine is fraught with sin and brokenness. The living of embodied life is filled with bodily complaints and false signals and imagination. We do not practice meditation "to do it right." We seek to be intentional and to practice it well. The intention in your heart and the willingness in your mind count. It is the "showing up" and "sitting" and "letting go" and "coming back" that matters.

Should I focus on my breath or a specific thought?

For most people, it begins with paying attention to the breath; but for others, it might be using a word, phrase, or gentle sound. For some, an icon will be a choice. Be bold and try different focuses for your meditation practice, finding out which helps you feel the most centered.

What if I start to feel anxious or overwhelmed?

It can be natural to feel unsettled or overwhelmed, especially in the beginning. Recognize this as a natural response, and acknowledge the feelings as they arise, allowing yourself to become more present through attentive breathing. You can also pause or stop the practice if you wish. Be kind to yourself, remember that things move at their own pace, and please, do not beat yourself up about how it goes.

Can I still practice if I do not believe in a higher power?

I have found through my conversations with other religious people and with non-believers in twelve-step programs that having some higher power is essential to life. This is your journey, and I do hope the book has helped you begin to resist in some way the forces of constant connectivity. Nevertheless, it might also be simply a practice for you. It might help you grow and evolve as a human being; it might help you become less reactionary. It might help you learn to respond more wisely; it might help you keep yourself centered when you experience intense emotions. It might help you to navigate the contemporary world in a way that is incredibly helpful and important, all without believing in a higher power.

I am a Christian. I believe there is more to creation than just you and your body. I believe in God, and through prayer, we can connect to this divine presence and spirit in the world. I hope that with contemplation, you will realize there is more to life than just yourself. You may discover that while you are worthy of belonging and love, you are, in fact, a part of creation. By connecting with others and finding community, you may understand how we are meant to be together and support each other. Over time, you may come to believe in a higher power and become curious about religion.

How often should I meditate to see results?

Any amount of time, even five to ten minutes daily, is a beginning step in practicing in the presence of God. Work up to ten minutes and then see how your body and mind respond, adding more time if you feel comfortable. The key is to be consistent. Regular, small efforts lead to meaningful and more positive experiences over time. Twenty minutes once a day will begin to reshape your life and ought to be a goal.

Is contemplative prayer only for monks or nuns?

No. This is a critical question. Contemplative prayer, the prayer of the heart, really has a home in the monastic life, but it is the prayer of every single human being. No one is excluded from it, but everyone is called upon to make time to still themselves and rest themselves in the presence of God, whether you are working hard in a profession, in service to others, if you have a busy family life, or are retired.

What if I am afraid of the silence?

It is understandable that some may feel nervous about it, particularly in a noisy, distracting world. Silence is intimidating—especially since the divine can use it to whisper wisdom to us. Part of this is learning there is nothing to fear in your thoughts and allowing them to float by, which itself can become healing. Some may feel an existential dread about being with their thoughts. There is a reality to this work that disempowers our hurried and crowded mind from its control over us. To control your thoughts is to create a backlog in your subconscious. The only way to deal with these overwhelming floods of thought is to release the dam. A spiritual direction and therapy can be assets if this is what you are experiencing. Getting to a place where you can allow yourself to rest in God's presence, knowing that God is there with you, stilling you, quieting you, is exactly this work.

Will contemplative prayer change me?

While contemplative prayer can and does effect change in our lives, more often than not, that change is subtle and understated. You might begin to experience greater peace or patience or, gradually, an even clearer sense of God and presence in your life and the lives of those you encounter. By making regular time for connection and quiet, for the Sabbath and embodied prayer, your heart and life will awaken to curiosity and possibility.

Is contemplative prayer safe for my spiritual life?

Yes, contemplative prayer is harmless and beneficial. It is about drawing closer to God and feeling the will of God more intensely. Any spiritual discipline can be practiced with the mindset of Christ, one that is open, humble, and trusting of God, anchored in God's Word, and guided by trusted spiritual mentors so that, in every moment, you remain Christ-centered in the most life-giving way.

What if I am not "good" at praying?

There is no such thing as being "good" or "bad" at prayer. Prayer, with words or without, is something that must be practiced. It is to open oneself to God, speak honestly, and be present. So often, we worry about the words to say. The brilliance of contemplative prayer is that words are not necessarily needed, while quietness is essential.

Glossary

The Internet of Things (IoT)

The Information Age can be divided into three distinct phases. The first phase was characterized by traditional media, such as newspapers, radio, and television. The second phase brought about the development of the Internet, satellites, computers, and mobile phones. The third phase emerged with the rise of social media, effectively merging elements from the first and second phases. The Information Age began in the late 1960s and early 1970s and officially concluded in 2020.

At the writing of this book, we are in the fourth year and the dawn of a new age. We now find ourselves in the Age of IoT, which will likely be remembered as the Age of Surveillance. The Internet of Things refers to a network of internet-enabled devices extending beyond traditional computers and smartphones to include various objects, such as automobiles, homes, televisions, and refrigerators. These interconnected devices continuously collect and transmit data over wireless networks without human intervention.

The term *Internet of Things* was first coined by Kevin Ashton in 1999 during his work at Procter & Gamble and now is applied to the whole new century. In this age, we seek to think differently. As we enter the Age of IoT, we borrow from the words of William Boeing, to "Build something better" (Korzec2020).

The Brain and the Mind

In this text, I use the term *brain* to mean the physical part of the body. I will join philosophers in using the term *mind* to speak of the place from which consciousness may be generated.

The Surveillance Age

Shoshana Zuboff describes this new era as that of a "Surveillance Age" in which pretty much everything we do is monitored and tracked, mainly by large private companies that want to know more about us—the things we search for online, the things we buy, and where and when we do it. Firms gather this information about us to influence or even control our choices—what might we buy next? What will make us click on that advertising link? According to Zuboff, this represents a new power that can influence our behavior without our consciously knowing it is happening.

Zuboff goes further: even as extensive data analyses of what we do worldwide, it also tracks what we might be about to do. By collecting mountains of data on people, companies can start to make educated guesses about what we might do next—and they can use this information to influence our choices in subtle ways. Such direct attempts to influence our choices using the data we generate, whether they do so to sell us products or nudge us toward habits or litigations, constitute a new and powerful way to exert control over our personal information and, therefore, over public spaces and domains. According to Zuboff, this has significant implications for our privacy and freedom.

Bibliography

Alper, B. A. (2023, December 7). *Spirituality among Americans*. Pew Research Center. https://www.pewresearch.org/religion/2023/12/07/spirituality-among-americans/.

American Psychological Association. (2017). *Stress in AmericaTM Poll*. https://www.apa.org/news/press/releases/2017/02/checking-devices#:~:text=Constant%20Checkers%20Experience%20Higher%20Stress&text=The%20survey%20found%20that%20stress,engage%20with%20technology%20as%20frequently.

Andrade, C., & Radhakrishnan, R. (2009). Prayer and healing: A medical and scientific perspective on randomized controlled trials. *Indian Journal of Psychiatry, 51*(4), 247. https://doi.org/10.4103/0019-5545.58288.

Anglican Consultative Council. (2008). *Lambeth conference resolutions and statements on the environment and climate change*. Anglican Alliance. https://anglicanalliance.org/lambeth-conference-resolutions-and-statements-on-the-environment-and-climate-change/#:~:text=The%20destruction%20of%20the%20environment,habits%20that%20are%20ecologically%20irresponsible.

Annie E. Casey Foundation. (2024, June 10). *Pandemic learning loss and Covid-19: Education impacts*. https://www.aecf.org/blog/pandemic-learning-loss-impacting-young-peoples-futures.

Anonymous. (1961). *The cloud of unknowing, translated into Modern English with an introduction by Clifton Wolters* (C. Wolters, Trans.). Penguin.

Argyris, J., Doltsinis, J. St., Fischer, H., & Wüstenberg, H. (1985). Ta πanta pei. *Computer Methods in Applied Mechanics and Engineering, 51*(1–3), 289–362. https://doi.org/10.1016/0045-7825(85)90038-6.

Augustine of Hippo. (2017). *Confessions* (S. Ruden, Trans.). Modern Library.

Barna Group. (2023a, August 16). *Caring for souls in a new reality: A barna webcast.* https://www.barna.com/research/caring-for-souls-webcast/.

Barna Group. (2023b, December 20). *Year in review: Barna's top 10 releases of 2020.* https://www.barna.com/research/year-in-review-2020/.

Baudrillard, J. (1994). *Simulacra and simulation* (S. F. Glaser, Trans.). The University of Michigan Press.

Berridge, K. C., & Robinson, T. E. (2016). Liking, wanting, and the incentive-sensitization theory of addiction. *American Psychologist, 71*(8), 670–79. https://doi.org/10.1037/amp0000059.

Blume, C., Garbazza, C., & Spitschan, M. (2019). Effects of light on human circadian rhythms, sleep and mood. *Somnologie, 23*(3), 147–56. https://doi.org/10.1007/s11818-019-00215-x.

Bonhoeffer, D. (2015). *Life together* (D. W. Bloesch, Trans.). Fortress Press.

Bourgeault, C. (2001). *Mystical hope: Trusting in the mercy of god.* Cowley Publications.

Bourgeault, C. (2003). *The wisdom way of knowing: Reclaiming an ancient tradition to awaken the heart.* Jossey-Bass.

Bourgeault, C. (2016). *The heart of centering prayer: Nondual Christianity in theory and practice.* Shambhala.

Bourgeault, C., & Keating, T. (2003). *Centering prayer and inner awakening.* Cowley Publications.

Burén, J., Nutley, S. B., & Thorell, L. B. (2023). Screen time and addictive use of gaming and social media in relation to health outcomes. *Frontiers in Psychology, 14.* https://doi.org/10.3389/fpsyg.2023.1258784.

Caldwell, P. (2006). *Finding you finding me: Using intensive interaction to get in touch with people whose severe learning disabilities are combined with autistic spectrum disorder.* Jessica Kingsley.

Carr, N. (2011). *The shallows: What the internet is doing to our brains.* Norton.

Cavanaugh, W. T. (2024). Marion on idolatry as a mirror to the self. In *The Uses of Idolatry* (pp. 190–216). Oxford University Press.

Cayley, D., Taylor, C., & Illich, I. (2015). *The rivers north of the future: The testament of Ivan Illich.* House of Anansi Press.

Chalmers, D. J. (2014). *The character of consciousness.* Oxford University Press.

Chen, H., Dong, G., & Li, K. (2023). Overview on brain function enhancement of internet addicts through exercise intervention: Based on reward-execution-decision cycle. *Frontiers in Psychiatry, 14.* https://doi.org/10.3389/fpsyt.2023.1094583.

Cilluffo, A. (2019, June 17). *World's population is projected to nearly stop growing by the end of the century.* Pew Research Center. https://www.pewresearch.org/short-reads/2019/06/17/worlds-population-is-projected-to-nearly-stop-growing-by-the-end-of-the-century/.

Cramer, H., Haller, H., Lauche, R., Steckhan, N., Michalsen, A., & Dobos, G. (2014). A systematic review and meta-analysis of yoga for hypertension. *American Journal of Hypertension, 27*(9), 1146–51. https://doi.org/10.1093/ajh/hpu078.

Crimmins, T. (2023, August 9). *"Do you see any diversity?": Man says AI is ABLEIST after generating 100-plus images of 'an autistic person'—and they're all white men.* The Daily Dot. https://www.dailydot.com/irl/ai-autistic-ableist/.

Damasio, A. (2008). *Descartes' error: Emotion, reason and the human brain.* Vintage Digital.

Davidson, R. J., Kabat-Zinn, J., Schumacher, J., Rosenkranz, M., Muller, D., Santorelli, S. F., Urbanowski, F., Harrington, A., Bonus, K., & Sheridan, J. F. (2003). Alterations in brain and immune function produced by mindfulness meditation. *Psychosomatic Medicine, 65*(4), 564–70. https://doi.org/10.1097/01.psy.0000077505.67574.e3.

Devi, K. A., & Singh, S. K. (2023). The hazards of excessive screen time: Impacts on physical health, mental health, and overall well-being. *Journal of Education and Health Promotion, 12*(1). https://doi.org/10.4103/jehp.jehp_447_23.

Diversity wins: How inclusion matters. Mckinsey & Co. (2020). https://www.mckinsey.com/~/media/mckinsey/featured insights/diversity and inclusion/diversity wins how inclusion matters/diversity-wins-how-inclusion-matters-vf.pdf

Eisenstein, C. (2013). *The ascent of humanity: Civilization and the human sense of self*. Evolver Editions.

Eldridge, R. (1993). Althusser and ideological criticism of the arts. *Explanation and Value in the Arts*, 190–214. https://doi.org/10.1017/cbo9780511659492.010.

Ellul, J. (1964). *The technological society* (J. Wilkinson, Trans.). Vintage Books.

Ersner-Hershfield, H., Wimmer, G. E., & Knutson, B. (2008). Saving for the future self: Neural measures of future self-continuity predict temporal discounting. *Social Cognitive and Affective Neuroscience, 4*(1), 85–92. https://doi.org/10.1093/scan/nsn042.

Fredrickson, B. L., Cohn, M. A., Coffey, K. A., Pek, J., & Finkel, S. M. (2008). Open hearts build lives: Positive emotions, induced through loving-kindness meditation, build consequential personal resources. *Journal of Personality and Social Psychology, 95*(5), 1045–62. https://doi.org/10.1037/a0013262.

Haidt, J. (2006). *The happiness hypothesis: Finding modern truth in ancient wisdom*. Basic Books.

Haidt, J. (2012). *The righteous mind: Why good people are divided by politics and religion*. Gildan Media, LLC.

Harari, Y. N. (2014). *Sapiens: A brief history of humankind*. Harper Collins.

Harari, Y. N. (2017). *Homo deus: A brief history of tomorrow*. HarperCollins.

Harenstam, T. (2015). Mobile phone use and mental health. A review of the research that takes a psychological perspective on exposure. *International Journal of Environmental Research and Public Health*. https://pubmed.ncbi.nlm.nih.gov/30501032/.

Harris, M. (2015). *The end of absence: Reclaiming what we've lost in a world of constant connection*. Current/Penguin Group.

Hart, D. B. (2004). *The beauty of the infinite: The aesthetics of Christian truth*. William B. Eerdmans.

Hart, D. B. (2011). *The Doors of the sea: Where was God in the tsunami?* William B. Eerdmans.

Hart, D. B. (2020). *Theological territories: A David Bentley Hart digest*. University of Notre Dame Press.

Hart, D. B. (2021). *That all shall be saved: Heaven, hell, and universal salvation: With a new preface*. Yale University Press.

Hart, D. B. (2024). *All things are full of gods: The mysteries of mind and life*. Yale University Press.

Harvard Health. (2024, July 24). *Blue light has a dark side*. Harvard Health. https://www.health.harvard.edu/staying-healthy/blue-light-has-a-dark-side.

Hull, J. M. (2002). *In the beginning there was darkness: A blind person's conversations with the Bible*. Trinity Press International.

Hull, J. (2017). *Notes on blindness: An experience of blindness*. Profile Books.

Illich, I. (1975). *Conviviality: Lecture, International Institute for Labour Studies*. International Institute for Labour Studies.

Illich, I. (1991). *Limits to medicine: Medical nemesis—the expropriation of health*. Penguin.

Illich, I. D. (1976). *Medical nemesis: The expropiation of health.* Pantheon Books.

Internet addiction, smartphone addiction, and Hikikomori trait in Japanese young adult: Social isolation and social network. *Frontiers in Psychiatry, 10.* https://doi.org/10.3389/fpsyt.2019.00455.

Ironson, G., & Ahmad, S. S. (2022). Praying for people you know predicts survival over 17 years among people living with HIV in the U.S. *Journal of Religion and Health, 61*(5), 4081–95. https://doi.org/10.1007/s10943-022-01622-5.

Kabat-Zinn, J. (1990). *Full catastrophe living.* Dell Publishing Co.

Kahneman, D. (2011). *Thinking, fast and slow.* Farrar, Straus and Giroux.

Kapor Center. (2017). Tech Leavers Study. https://www.kaporcenter.org/wp-content/uploads/2017/08/TechLeavers2017.pdf.

Kaufmann, C. (2024, May 29). *The digital divide.* Pew Charitable Trusts. https://www.pewtrusts.org/en/trust/archive/spring-2024/the-digital-divide.

Kemp, S. (2024, January 31). *Digital 2024: Global Overview Report—DataReportal—Global Digital Insights.* DataReportal. https://datareportal.com/reports/digital-2024-global-overview-report

Korzec, M. D. (2020, October 31). *IOT.* Medium. https://medium.com/swlh/iot-a7fd31445902

LaBar, K. S., & Phelps, E. A. (1998). Arousal-mediated memory consolidation: Role of the medial temporal lobe in humans. *Psychological Science, 9*(6), 490–93. https://doi.org/10.1111/1467-9280.00090.

Lasn, K. (1999). *Culture jam: The uncooling of America.* Morrow Publishing.

Lasn, K. (2013). *Meme wars. The creative destruction of neoclassical economics.* Seven Stories Press.

Lazar, S. W., Kerr, C. E., Wasserman, R. H., Gray, J. R., Greve, D. N., Treadway, M. T., McGarvey, M., Quinn, B. T.,

Dusek, J. A., Benson, H., Rauch, S. L., Moore, C. I., & Fischl, B. (2005). Meditation experience is associated with increased cortical thickness. *NeuroReport, 16*(17), 1893–97. https://doi.org/10.1097/01.wnr.0000186598.66243.19.

Lissak, G. (2018). Adverse physiological and psychological effects of screen time on children and adolescents: Literature review and case study. *Environmental Research, 164*, 149–57. https://doi.org/10.1016/j.envres.2018.01.015.

Marion, J.-L. (2020). *The crossing of the visible* (J. Smith, Trans.). Stanford University Press.

Mark, G. (2014, November 25). *Click bait is a distracting affront to our focus*. Informatics @ the University of California, Irvine. https://www.informatics.uci.edu/2014/11/.

Matamoros-Fernández, A., & Farkas, J. (2021). Racism, hate speech, and Social Media: A systematic review and Critique. Television & New Media, 22(2), 205–224. https://doi.org/10.1177/1527476420982230 Maté, D., & Maté, D. (2022). *The myth of normal: Trauma, illness, and healing in a toxic culture*. Penguin Publishing Group.

McLaren, B. (2011, September 24). *We're connected by what we eat*. Sojourners. https://sojo.net/articles/were-connected-what-we-eat.

Merleau-Ponty, M. (1994). Phenomenology of Perception. Routledge & Kegan Paul.

Mennella, C., Maniscalco, U., De Pietro, G., & Esposito, M. (2024). Ethical and regulatory challenges of AI technologies in healthcare: A narrative review. *Heliyon, 10*(4). https://doi.org/10.1016/j.heliyon.2024.e26297.

Merton, T. (1986). *Seeds of contemplation*. New Directions Pub. Corp.

Mizuno, J., & Monteiro, H. L. (2013). An assessment of a sequence of yoga exercises to patients with arterial hypertension. *Journal of Bodywork and Movement Therapies, 17*(1), 35–41. https://doi.org/10.1016/j.jbmt.2012.10.007.

Morris, W. (2016). *Theology without words: Theology in the deaf community*. Taylor and Francis.

Nagare, R., Rea, M. S., Plitnick, B., & Figueiro, M. G. (2019, April). Nocturnal melatonin suppression by adolescents and adults for different levels, spectra, and durations of light exposure. *Journal of Biological Rhythms*. https://www.ncbi.nlm.nih.gov/pmc/articles/PMC6640648/.

Newberg, A. B. (2014). The neuroscientific study of spiritual practices. *Frontiers in Psychology, 5*. https://doi.org/10.3389/fpsyg.2014.00215.

Nhất Hạnh, T. trans.Kotler, A. (1991). *Peace is every step: The path of mindfulness in everyday life*. Bantam Books.

Noble, S. U. (2018). *Algorithms of Oppression: How search engines reinforce racism*. NYU Press.

Owens, B. (2024, September 18). Rage against machine learning driven by profit. Nature News. https://www.nature.com/articles/d41586-024-02985-3

Oxford Internet Institute. (2019). *The global disinformation order: 2019 global inventory of organised social media manipulation*. https://www.oii.ox.ac.uk/news-events/reports/the-global-disinformation-order-2019-global-inventory-of-organised-social-media-manipulation.

Page, C., & Bourgeault, C. (2013, April 22). *Cynthia Bourgeault—"contemplative remembering" #2*. In A Spacious Place. https://inaspaciousplace.wordpress.com/2013/04/18/cynthia-bourgeault-contemplative-remembering-2/.

Pedersen, J., Rasmussen, M. G., Sørensen, S. O., Mortensen, S. R., Olesen, L. G., Brage, S., Kristensen, P. L., Puterman, E., & Grøntved, A. (2022). Effects of limiting digital screen use on well-being, mood, and biomarkers of stress in adults. *Npj Mental Health Research, 1*(1). https://doi.org/10.1038/s44184-022-00015-6.

Prensky, M. (2001, September 1). *Digital Natives, digital immigrants part 1*. On the Horizon. https://www.emerald.com/insight/content/doi/10.1108/10748120110424816/full/html.

Putnam, R. D. (2001). *Bowling alone: The collapse and revival of American community*. Touchstone.

Putnam, R. D. (2020). *Bowling alone: The collapse and revival of American community*. Simon & Schuster Paperbacks.

Raymond, J., Varney, C., Parkinson, L. A., & Gruzelier, J. H. (2005). The effects of alpha/theta neurofeedback on personality and mood. *Cognitive Brain Research, 23*(2–3), 287–92. https://doi.org/10.1016/j.cogbrainres.2004.10.023.

Robert, S. J., & Kadhiravan, S. (2022). Prevalence of digital amnesia, somatic symptoms and sleep disorders among youth during COVID-19 pandemic. *Heliyon, 8*(8). https://doi.org/10.1016/j.heliyon.2022.e10026.

Rohr, R. (2021). *The universal Christ: How a forgotten reality can change everything we see, hope for, and believe*. Convergent.

Rule of the SSJE. (1997). Cowley Publications.

Ryle, G. (1949). *The Concept of Mind*. University of Chicago Press.

Sacks, J. (2023, September 6). *The art of listening: Bereishit: Covenant & conversation*. The Rabbi Sacks Legacy. https://rabbisacks.org/covenant-conversation/bereishit/the-art-of-listening/.

https://www.scientificamerican.com/article/american-consumption-habits/.

Simondon, G. (2007). *Physico-Biological Genesis of the Individual* (T. Adkins, Trans.). Presses universitaires de France.

Simondon, G., Malaspina, C., & Rogove, J. (2017). *On the mode of existence of technical objects*. Univocal Publishing.

Speranza, L., di Porzio, U., Viggiano, D., de Donato, A., & Volpicelli, F. (2021). Dopamine: The neuromodulator of long-term synaptic plasticity, reward and movement control. *Cells, 10*(4), 735. https://doi.org/10.3390/cells10040735.

Sting. (1981, October 2). *Sting: Discography: Ghost in the Machine*. Sting.com. https://www.sting.com/discography/album/32/The%20Police.

Stringfellow, W. (1973). *An ethic for Christians and other aliens in a strange land. William Stringfellow*. Creative Resources.

Stringfellow, W. (1977). *Conscience and obedience*. Word Books.

Subsplash and Barna. (2022). *Two trends that Reshaped Ministry in 2022*. Subsplash. https://subsplash.com/demos/media/mi/+d9jcz53

Thoreau, H. D. (1995). *Walden: An annotated edition* (W. Harding, Ed.). Houghton Mifflin.

Tipler, F. J. (1994). *The physics of immortality*. Random House.

Tolkien, J. R. R. (1978). *The lord of the rings*. Houghton Mifflin.

UN Environmental Programme. (2024). *Global resources outlook 2024*. UNEP. https://www.unep.org/resources/Global-Resource-Outlook-2024.

Vardey, L., & Theresa, M. (1995). *A simple path*. Ballentine.

Vogels, E. A. (2021, January 13). *The state of online harassment*. Pew Research Center. https://www.pewresearch.org/internet/2021/01/13/the-state-of-online-harassment/.

Vorster-De Wet, R., Gerber, A. M., & Raubenheimer, J. E. (2023). Effect of receiving mobile text messages on cortisol concentrations in students at the University of the Free State. *Health SA Gesondheid, 28*. https://doi.org/10.4102/hsag.v28i0.2064

Walker, R. T., & Torrance, T. F. (2008). *Incarnation: The person and life of Christ. Edited by Robert T. Walker*. IVP Academic.

Weil, S. (1979). *Waiting on God*. Routledge.

White supremacist propaganda incidents soar to record high in 2023. ADL. (2023, March 8). https://www.adl.org/resources/report/white-supremacist-propaganda-incidents-soar-record-high-2023

WHO. (2020). *The true death toll of COVID-19 estimating global excess mortality*. World Health Organization. https://www.who.int/data/stories/the-true-death-toll-of-covid-19-estimating-global-excess-mortality

WHO. (2021). *The top 10 causes of death*. World Health Organization. https://www.who.int/news-room/fact-sheets/detail/the

-top-10-causes-of-death#:~:text=Leading%20causes%20of%20death%20in,9.1%20million%20deaths%20in%202021.

World Health Organization. (n.d.). *Covid-19 cases | WHO COVID-19 Dashboard*. World Health Organization. https://data.who.int/dashboards/covid19/cases

Williams, R. (2009). *Tokens of trust an introduction to Christian belief*. TPB.

Williams, R. (2011). *Silence and honey cakes: The wisdom of the desert*. Lion Hudson.

Williams, R. (2014a). *Being Christian: Baptism, Bible, Eucharist, prayer*. William B. Eerdmans Publishing Company.

Williams, R. (2014b). *On Christian theology*. Alexander Street Press.

Williams, R. (2014c). *The wound of knowledge*. Darton Longman & Todd.

Williams, R. (2015). *Faith in the public square*. Bloomsbury Continuum.

Williams, R. L. (2021). *Bonhoeffer's black Jesus: Harlem Renaissance theology and an ethic of resistance*. Baylor University Press.

World Data Lab. (2024). *Internet poverty index*. Internet Poverty Index. https://internetpoverty.io/.

Yates, M. (2021). Instrumental reason. In *Cambridge Habermas Lexicon* (pp. 197–99). Cambridge University Press.

Yong, A. (2020). *Theology and down Syndrome: Reimagining disability in late modernity*. Baylor University Press.

Zheng, D., Berry, D. R., & Brown, K. W. (2023). Effects of brief mindfulness meditation and compassion meditation on parochial empathy and prosocial behavior toward ethnic out-group members. *Mindfulness, 14*(10), 2454–70. https://doi.org/10.1007/s12671-023-02100-z.

Zimbardo, P., & Boyd, J. (2010). *The time paradox: Using the new psychology of time to your advantage*. Rider.

Zubair, U., Khan, M. K., & Albashari, M. (2023). Link between excessive social media use and psychiatric disorders. *Annals of Medicine & Surgery, 85*(4), 875–78. https://doi.org/10.1097/ms9.0000000000000112.

Zuboff, S. (2020). *The age of surveillance capitalism: The fight for a human future at the New Frontier of Power*. PublicAffairs.

About the Author

C. Andrew Doyle has been the ninth Bishop of Texas for over a decade. During that time the Diocese of Texas has grown, and he now oversees and pastors more than 78,000 parishioners and 400 clergy working in 163 congregations, 91 missional communities, 21 campus missions, 57 schools, and 10 institutions. Bishop Doyle received his M.Div. from Virginia Theological Seminary after receiving a fine arts degree from the University of North Texas. Previous to his election in 2008, Bishop Doyle served for five years as Canon to the Ordinary. He also served in churches in Temple and College Station, and was elected deputy to several General Conventions. He most recently served on the Structure Committee and is currently president of the Compass Rose Society, a global group of patrons and leaders making a difference in the Anglican Communion. He has led the creation of two new foundations. He is known for his creative and strategic thinking, his advocacy for the immigrant and migrant, his work in stewardship and development, and most recently for the creation of a Racial Justice initiative with a $13 million corpus.

He describes his six-word autobiography as: "Met Jesus on pilgrimage, still walking." Bishop Doyle's focus for ministry is challenging Episcopalians to move into their communities with the Gospel in word and action. He is a preacher, a teacher, and a speaker. He has been interviewed on CBS, in *Newsweek*, in *Texas Monthly*, and for *Wired*. His teaching mixes references from pop culture's music and movies with the latest in secular leadership trends in order to reach the broadest spectrum of readers.

His books include *Unabashedly Episcopalian: The Good News of the Episcopal Church*, 2012; *Orgullosamente Episcopal*, 2015; *Church: A Generous Community Amplified for the Future*, 2015; *A Generous Community: Being Church in a New Missionary Age*, 2015; *Small Batch: Local, Organic, and Sustainable Church*, 2016; *The Jesus Heist*, 2017; *Vocātiō: Imaging a Visible Church*, 2018; *Citizen: Faithful Discipleship in a Partisan World*, 2020; *Embodied Liturgy*, 2021; and *Episcopate*, 2023.

Bishop Doyle is married to JoAnne Doyle, and they have two daughters. He is a vinyl collector, reader, artist, banjo player, and fly fisherman.